Cover picture:

Bob and Pythagoras about to cross the Oubangui River on the Quinquemaran!

THROUGH

EBOLA

TERRITORY

A young couple with their 7-week-old son in a Malawian Fish Basket drive across 1971 war-devastated Zaire. They risk the hazards of jungle, swamp, guerrillas, insects, and wild animals. All round simmer Ebola and many other diseases, but the travellers' adventures deliver a lot of fun.

DAPHNE

In fide vade

INTRODUCTION

Until 1976 no one knew that Ebola was suppurating in the Congo's overpowering forests and bubbling in its sweltering marshes. In fact, nobody had even heard of the frightful disease. But it, and equally unknown AIDS, had been thriving there for years!

If you'd like to read bald, bloody facts about Ebola they are in the Appendix on page 181

When Bob, Daphne and Bruce crossed Zaire in 1971, years of vicious warfare and savage atrocities had devastated the country. Its amenities were razed or abandoned. Railways had vanished beneath rampant jungle; roads, overwhelmed by tangled vegetation, were eroded by constant rain. There were no buses, no trains... and private transport was almost unknown, so very little movement took place within the Congo. Ebola could, and did, wipe out the inhabitants of a hamlet here and a village there before a dugout splashed by on the river, or an occasional beer lorry blundered its way past through dense undergrowth.

With no motive for canoe or lorry to stop in a settlement without survivors, the virus was not picked up and carried on. That small outbreak fizzled out. Later, introduced by bats, rats or other carriers, another Ebola puffball would erupt elsewhere and when all *its* victims had expired, with no more people to infect, it died too. So again the sickness was not spread. Humanity was lucky – then! These days people travel about. They move not only between villages but also from country to country. So the foul plague is transported and transmitted. It explodes. Thousands of sufferers have died in recent years and in 2014 hundreds more victims fell ill *every day.*

****

ABOUT THE AUTHOR

Born in Egypt to an English-French family Daphne Heyring lived in various parts of Africa and the Middle East during times of stirring political events. She revelled in a varied and exciting life which regularly included driving to remote and dangerous regions, often camping under difficult conditions.

Her family were helpful to King Farouk, and later were friends of, and worked with, Haile Selassie (Emperor of Ethiopia) and his relations. As a young woman living alone in Addis Ababa Daphne kept her own horses; experienced breathtaking events in the Ethiopian attempted coup d'état; and braved bandit-infested regions to discover a route to the top of the highest mountain in Ethiopia.

In the days when Kibo Peak was still encrusted with deep snow and enormous ice cliffs she climbed Kilimanjaro not only to the top but also right into the then seldom-visited triple crater. During her first ascent in 1961 there were in all 6 people on the whole mountain. When (on her third ascent in 1984) she took up her son, Bruce, the Fish Basket baby, there were 200 climbers in just the middle refuge.

In her GP14 sailing dinghy on vast Lake Malawi, Daphne and her friends camped on islands so deserted that animals and birds, unafraid of humans, roamed between their tents. She always loved many varied furred and feathered pets including a monkey, who shared her delight in horse riding!

After secondary school and university in the UK, she was a university lecturer, teacher and headmistress, and now lives in an eccentric villa in Mallorca where she is an active member of various cultural societies. She enjoys imparting Scottish

Country Dancing to enthusiastic Majorcans, photography, strenuous mountain walking, swimming, gardening, and until recently – windsurfing. She has sold oil and watercolour paintings.

Daphne married Robert Martin, a Scottish Chartered Accountant. They have a son, Bruce.

She has several books pending publication and has written for Mountain Club and Scientific Journals.

****

0. Right round the bend. 2013. (Not on the website.)
Bruce took this shot of Daphne in the Mallorcan Mountains.

Dedication

This book is for Bruce, the Fish Basket Baby who turned into a wonderful son, to 'remind' him of what he once got up to!

2. The picture shows him *beside* his Fish Basket in February 2009 on the lawn of our Blantyre house where he grew up. By then he had rather outstripped his erstwhile cradle!

It's fun to compare this snap with photo number 48 (on page 177) of Bruce *in* his Fish Basket. But don't worry: this book isn't about the baby. He was with us, of course, because we couldn't exactly leave the Brat behind! But he doesn't feature much in the narrative.

****

Apart from the Guardian Angels, who appear very briefly in the first chapter, this book is non-fiction.

Although, obviously, I can't now remember the actual words, conversations throughout have been rendered to suit their situations.

First edition May 2015
Second edition July 2015

ISBN-13: 978-1511416085
ISBN-10: 1511416084

CONTENTS

CONTENTS continued

****

Illustrations

I digitised my old slides but the price of the book would have been astronomical if I had left them in colour. I had to put them into B&W in order to reduce the cost.

However, if you want to view the pics in colour, and see a few extra photos as well, go to www.daphne.es and follow the menu to Thru Ebola Territory or go straight to www.daphne.es/thru ebola territory

The pictures in this edition are numbered according to their order in the *first* edition of the printed book. For this edition I have re-positioned the pictures to be more convenient for the reader so numbering of pictures in this book is not sequential. On the website any extra pic has an E after its number.

Illustrations continued

****

OPTIONAL READ.

If you're not interested in times past then skip this 'teaspoon' of history and turn to Chapter One (on page 1). There the story really starts and everything becomes more light-hearted.

A bit of background about The Congo.

Perhaps you know all about the two countries in the middle of Africa which, between them, and at various times, have been called: Congo, Congo Free State, Zaire, Congo Brazzaville, Congo Leopoldville, The Democratic Republic of Congo, D.C.R., Kongo, The Belgian Congo etc. You may even understand which is which, and which has mutated into which. If so, I congratulate you. You are a very rare person.

If on the other hand, like me, you have only the haziest ideas about that huge morass in Africa's umbilical area – well – that's fine. As you've survived till now without much knowledge of its confused politics, dreadful climate and ferocious, constant wars, you'll probably continue to thrive perfectly happily without embarking upon an in-depth study of the region. However – superficially – it's interesting to know that the Congo Basin is blessed and cursed by enormous resources of commodities such as copper, gold, silver, diamonds... as well as the potential for incredible hydroelectric generation. The Hiroshima bomb used Congolese uranium. Exportable tea, coffee, quinine, flowers, tropical fruits and vegetables flourish – when not razed by wars.

Early in the 20th century the French grabbed the section west of the Congo River, whereas King Leopold II of Belgium seized the much larger eastern portion, and turned it into a vast personal domain.

In both provinces the inhabitants became slaves, who were starved, treated atrociously and forced to milk their own countries of their ample and varied natural resources in order to pour wealth into French coffers or into the regal pocket. Only if you see films of that epoch can you realise the apocalyptic cruelty of the locals' suffering.

Centred on brutal extraction of the raw materials, economic development boomed from 1908 to 1958 producing splendid roads, trains, airports, cities, and efficient agricultural estates. There were first-class establishments of all kinds. Neighbouring countries envied, and therefore invaded, the Congo's richness, so local wars erupted. Western powers intervened. The eastern and southern borders of Zaire became, and still are, running sores: the ongoing aftermath of continuing battles. Just about everything collapsed but ghastly endemic diseases prospered.

After gaining independence both countries called themselves 'The Republic of Congo' so they became known as 'Congo Brazzaville' (West) and 'Congo Leopoldville' (East). Over the years they had other appellations as listed above.

When my husband, Bob, and I, together with Bruce, our just-born son ensconced in a Malawian Fish Basket, bashed our Land Rover through its thick Equatorial jungle, the eastern domain was called Zaire. We were naïve to the point of madness about the conditions we would meet.

****

3. Bob, Daphne, and Bruce beside Pythagoras just before starting. Bruce seems to have mislaid a leg and a foot but, as you can see in picture 2, he does, in fact, have the normal complement of limbs and digits! The plastic 'clean-nappy bag' is seen through the window. Lying on the ground, it served as mattress for Bruce at lunch times, and otherwise was tucked over a carton of provisions in (vain) attempt to prevent the contents flying out when we went over big bumps or fell into deep holes.
Photo by Dr Hart of Malamulo Hospital, Blantyre.

Down in the jungle,
living in a tent –
Better than the prefabs – no rent!

(Old chant, popular in the time of prefabricated houses after World War II.)

21E. Lake Kivu, showing some of the 'inland islands'.

Please remember that you can see the pictures in colour by going to www.daphne.es and then selecting Thru Ebola Territory. On that website you'll also find other stories that you can read.

6. Possible Ebola carriers

In the Guinean forest there is a bare and blasted tree trunk bleached by lightning. It has an ominous look and it is the country's 'Ground Zero' because Ebola first appeared in Guinea when bats living in that hollow relic were caught by small boys and eaten by villagers.

CHAPTER ONE

Twice lucky

Zaire was a shambles – a mess left after war. Throughout its incredibly dense equatorial jungle marauding desperados, killed and looted. Rusting military vehicles rotted in destroyed, shrapnel-scarred settlements, and there was virtually no traffic on tortured stretches of mud that passed for roads. We didn't know it would be like this. But we couldn't turn back. We had to struggle on to reach Europe before my gravely ill parents died.

'Station de L'Epulu' was another war-torn village yet still visible was an ancient, lopsided sign advertising "Pygmy village and Game Park with Exotic Animals". We decided to view these marvels – if they still existed – and then to camp nearby, beside a beautiful bend of the local river. Our map told us it was the Ebola, a distant tributary of the Congo.

But when we stopped beside the placard we were met not by a uniformed game guard but by a scruffy, distracted-looking woman.

"Where's the Warden?" we asked.

In very accented French she replied:

"She is died."

"We would like to see the Pygmies."

"She is died."

"The village seems very empty. Where are all the people?"

"She is died."

It seemed to be all she could utter. This was depressing and odd but we dutifully paid 1 Zaire each (then worth about 14/-) and extracted the baby from his basket because...

"To see animals," said the lady in a dead voice," must proceed with feet."

How thrilling! In most game parks visitors were never allowed out of their cars. Indeed, we did advance under our own steam – for about 50 metres (!) but only to shockingly small cages containing 1 mongoose, 1 small crocodile, 2 bongos – and that was *it*! Game Park indeed! Badly maintained tiny zoo more like! Deciding to recoup what we could of the swindle and record the bongo anyway we hauled out cameras. Consternation! To take photos a further Zaire had to be paid! A slanging match did no good except that, while Bob argued, I was able to click once – very surreptitiously.

No Pygmies – no game wardens – cages! – no collection of exciting animals – no photos – a most uncouth 'guide'...?
"Why did they all die?"
The woman shrugged. In her appalling French, with horribly explicit and repulsive actions to illustrate her meaning, she replied:
"She is died. Too much diarrhoea. Vomit bad. Plenty blood."
Classic Ebola symptoms – had we but known. Whatever it was, it sounded vile. Coughing and sneezing, she didn't sound at all well herself!

Retiring to the car in high dungeon we were gripped by a sudden unaccountable sense of foreboding so we didn't hang about. Heading straight off, angry, disappointed and uncharacteristically edgy, we didn't do justice to the multitude of birds on the riverbanks or to the beauty of that spot where Fish Eagles 'laughed' and doves were cooing a typical African melody. Years later we learnt that it was an outbreak of Ebola which had caused the deaths. We were very lucky to get such a bad impression that, instead of lingering, we sped away from Station de L'Epulu without contacting anyone except the awful 'guide'.

Some hours on we had another lucky escape. We tried to locate the road to Isiro Village (where Ebola was even then taking its toll and close to where it was finally studied in 1976). From there, according to the map, our proposed route eventually led out of Zaire and into Central African Republic! But, like other 'highways' we had tried to use, that track's plant-infested surface could barely be seen. Giant trees lay haphazardly across unimaginably deep ruts. So instead of bouncing *north*wards towards Europe we were forced to follow the one available (only slightly less appalling) trail, which took us *west southwest*. Consequently, although we passed through Ebola-infested Isiro *District* we never reached Isiro *Village* and thus fortuitously avoided yet another spot where death was wiping out the population.

That night our guardian angels must have exchanged meaningful looks and emitted a resounding: "PHEW!"
Perhaps they then said:
"So.... wot´s next blummin call-out wi gonna get d'ya fink?"
"Nay, I dunno. Nowt surprises me nowadays. Thai seem to have a death wish an ´ave got it inter thair ´eads to motor up ´ole o' this 'ere continent an all."
"For starters, this lot ´ave git thersens deep inter Ebola territory. Bonkers I call it."
"I reckon thai gonna end up ahead where´t vomit and diarrhoea's in full flow right now."
"D'yer fink that splutterin´ woman passed it on wiv ´er spittin´ all o´er?"
"Huh, if she 'as, thai'll all be gonners afor´t month's out coz thiz no even clinics in this neck o´t woods. Thai need to gerrout o Zaire to get near a nospital an´ that´s hellova way. Thai'v no chance."
"Hey man, that´s worra reelly like about yer. Yer allus full a optimism."
"Well, it ain´t funny. We flog oursens almost to death watchin´ o´er these barmpots an´ yer know ther's no quacks ken cure ut. So an´ they gerrit, they die."
"Yer right, but chill out man an´ look on´t brightside – if thai all die, me an' you´ll ´ave an easier life.
"True, but hey! Watch it! Looks like yer´ve got another job on this blimmin' second – that daft woman o´er yonder finks that snake's a bit o kindlin."

****

Had we been lucky because that happened on the *thirteenth* day of our trip up the length of Africa? It was 3rd November 1971, but our epic really had its beginnings four years earlier.

7. Our entire trip, which is recorded in *The Daftest Journey.*

1 & 18 Malawi; 2 & 17 Zambia; 3 & T Tanzania;
4 Burundi; 5 Rwanda; 6 Zaire; 7 C.A.R.; 8 Cameroon;
9 Nigeria; 10 Niger; 11 Algeria; 12 Spain; 13 France; 14 UK;
15 S. Africa; 16 Rhodesia; M Mozambique; S Sudan; C Chad.

CHAPTER TWO

How it started.

Ted shattered a thoughtful silence with an accusation:
"You're a university lecturer, not a flippin' motor mechanic!"
I looked him in the eye.
"So?"
"So why are you spending every Monday to Friday of your long vacation working at the VW garage?"
"I'm working as one of the apprentices to learn absolutely all there is to know about Beetles."
"Why – for goodness sakes?" asked Bob.
I sighed. It would have to come out sooner or later.
"I'm hoping to drive to Europe."
"What! From *here*? – Rhodesia!" Ted's voice sounded squeaky with incredulity.
"Yes. I'll need to know how to fix my car of it breaks down."
"You won't have the strength to manage some repairs," observed Bob sapiently.
"But if I carry spare torsion bars and so on there will be people in villages with the brute strength to do what I ask them to."
"You're mad!" declared Ted, going pale.
"It could be a fine adventure," hesitated Bob. He wanted to stay in my good books because he had asked me to marry him and I was stalling. That's how it started.

Time passed. I knew the route to Ethiopia but after that I'd have to cross the Nubian Desert. The idea was a bit daunting so I wasn't altogether heartbroken when tribal conflicts in The Sudan kept on making travel impossible.

Bob and I married and moved to Malawi. From there we revelled in extended safaris in our short-wheel-base Land Rover. An old model, innocent of any streamlining, he was all sharp right angles, so we called him 'Pythagoras'. Besides, his number, BC 585, was very nearly the year of the great mathematician's birth. The actual date was probably BC 580;

but what does a mere plus or minus 5 matter in these circumstances?

One day Bob suggested:

"You know the route to Europe doesn't *have* to go up the *east* of Africa."

In 1970 there seemed a chance that fighting in the Congo might be easing. In English and French we wrote off for visas to enter, cross and leave 13 African countries and began to prepare Pythagoras for the great expedition. My Beetle would not be coming. All that hard work in the VW garage... It wouldn't be much help if the *Land Rover* collapsed.

On the map, by running your finger roughly two-thirds of the way down the eastern side of Africa you'll find Malawi (numbers 1 & 18). From that country's commercial capital – Blantyre – we began the journey that stressed our guardian angels to the limit. As shown on the map our ambition was to drive to Scotland, take a passenger ship to Cape Town and complete our crossing of the Dark Continent by motoring from the Cape back north to Blantyre.

Through Ebola Territory is the account of a small part of that incredible odyssey. the ten tough, nail-biting days during which we crossed Zaire – as the Congo was then called.

The squad of worthies propping up the bar at Blantyre Club came from various parts of the globe, all walks of life and between them were experts in everything to do with Africa. But they were not renowned for tact. In a variety of accents they had a Field Day trumpeting their opinions:

"Heard what they're planning?

"It's crazy! Utterly *ridiculous*!"

"Well, I don't know... Conditions in South Africa are pretty good."

"Oh yes. They'll manage Cape Town to Rhodesia O.K., but that's just a tiny part of their entire trip. What about Mozambique? Our neighbour, you know – between Rhodesia and Malawi. We've all heard what things are like down there: terrorists, atrocities, constant explosions..."

"Hm."

(Oil painting 4.5ft X 8ft)

15. Cricket at Blantyre Club- The Old Codgers' stamping ground.

"We enjoyed a safari in Kenya last year... Of course we only used tracks that were well known..."
"That's the point. The blithering idiots won't *be* on beaten tracks. They're not going through well-known regions where tourists are accepted. Don't you get it? They're proposing to drive the *whole length of Africa,* man – the whole blinking way from south to north! And that's impossible!"
"Simply unheard of!"
"They'll have to bash through really wild terrain. Totally demented! That's what they are!"
"Did you hear that BBC report about cannibals the other day? – in Central African Republic?"
"Terrifying!"
"Creepy crawlies, leopards... "
"My sister's a missionary in Kisangani – that's one of the towns in the Congo. Says conditions there are simply frightful and they never go out of town because all facilities have been destroyed by wars, and the forests are full of gun- and machete-toting bandits."
"Ah – The Congo – I had to fly a recce over that not so long ago. Terrible place: huge mass of tangled, dirty green; enormous country – largest in Africa after the Sudan. Appeared to be a colossal compost heap."
"What about the rivers?"
"Oodles of 'em! Like tremendous, writhing snakes... orangey-brown slime. Biggest watercourse system in the world – more complex even than the Amazon"
"Decent bridges?"
"You must be joking! Rafts if you're lucky, man!"
"They'll never make it."
"Well, Bob won't. He's only just over *years* of that dysentery thing..."
"Thin as a stick insect... "
"And, did you hear? He had to have his appendix out last week."
"No! But they're planning to leave *next* week."

"Never mind about Bob. What about Daphne? She's only just given birth. She'll never be strong enough to cope with all the demands of such a strenuous journey."
"And the wretched babe. How will *that* cope?"
"Oh! It'll die, sure as eggs. I mean – jolted and bumped incessantly. Won't be able to sterilise its food when they're camping, for goodness sakes."
"D'you know – she actually made the tent herself? ... and heaps of other stuff as well... Stark staring bonkers!"
"But you can't *get* proper equipment here in Malawi. We continually *have* to improvise."
"Yes. I s'pose so."
"Lots of endemic diseases: malaria, dengue fever, bilharzias, cholera, typhoid... Rabies *everywhere*– naturally.
"One of 'em's bound to fall ill and scupper the whole trip."
"They'll regret it."
"Don't be daft. Can't regret anything when you're dead!"
"Not only *them* – the *vehicle* will probably break an axle or develop electrical troubles. No one negotiates those terrible trails without having an accident, y'know."
"They'll be stuck for days, or weeks even – that is, if guerrillas don't axe them to pulp and steal what they can take."
"Hey, Justin, where are you? Stop serving MGTs (Malawi Gin and Tonics) for a second and bring us the gambling book. Come on. Enter two wagers:
1 How long before the whole expedition founders?
2 Which of the four – counting the car – will collapse first and trigger a domino conk-out effect?"
Betting was thick, fast, and pessimistic about our prospects.

Club Codgers were right to be concerned. The difficulties of the trip were such that we should never have attempted it – especially not with a baby! It's hard for people these days to even imagine our antics on this journey as we overcame incredible conditions. They provoked many thrilling episodes and plenty of amusement

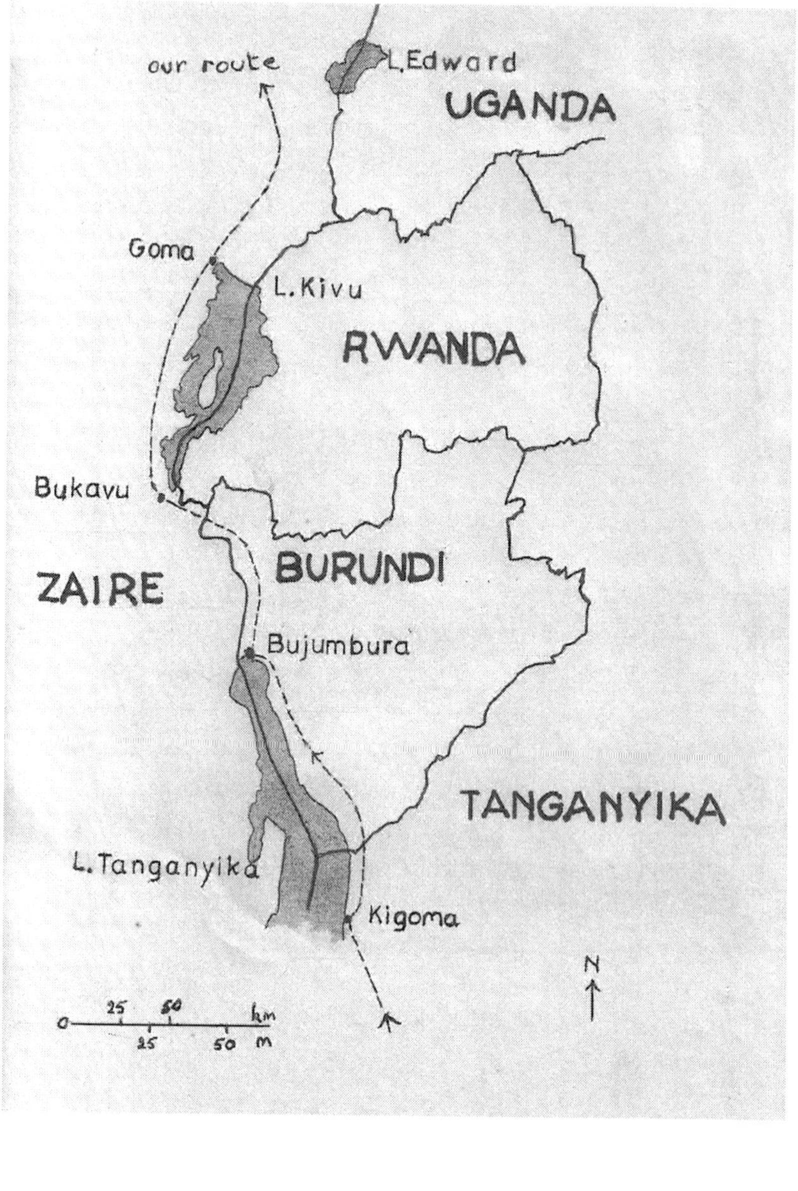

18. Our route from Kigoma (Tanganyika) through Burundi to Bukavu (Zaire) then northwards across the south of Northeast Zaire.

CHAPTER THREE

Ignorant of terrible news.

A most useful device.

Although we enjoyed the trip's numerous excitements – well – most of them! – looking back I can only suggest that we had taken leave of our senses. It wasn't a temporary aberration either. We'd had plenty of time to change our minds. We must have been not only demented but very determined because 10 months passed before we finished accumulating the essential documents and had acquired the extra-heavy-duty tyres and strongest possible springs as well as other very specialised apparatus that would be needed.

It was during those 10 months that I fell pregnant.

"We'll have to give up the whole scheme," said Bob, despondently.

But I wasn't having any of that:

"The Boers traipsed across Africa in wagons with entire families. We're not going to let one tiny brat affect our plans!"

Our start was delayed - but we *went*: innocent, ignorant, full of optimism *and with a nappy bucket under our feet.*

Only later did we learn that as we breakfasted on the morning of our departure, an ambulance was scuttling through the tortuous streets of Palma de Mallorca. In their Palma Nova flat, 14 km away, my parents, Florrie and Alec Heyring, waited. She was tense, pale and worried. He was ashen with pain. In Spain relatives were expected to stay with hospitalised patients to attend to physical needs, so at her feet a small suitcase contained necessities. She wondered whether her dicey heart would allow her to cope. It was already fluttering much too fast and irregularly. She thought of her daughter, now travelling across Africa and therefore beyond contact. Her mind strayed to the new baby. She and Alec had keenly followed details of the pregnancy's progress and their delight at Bruce's birth had been unbounded. Her husband was so much looking forward to cuddling the baby. But now he was desperately ill! Would he live to see their grandchild? Florrie's thoughts returned to her present predicament. Neither of her sons, one in England, the other in Nigeria, could take leave from his job. Both their wives were fully occupied with infants. No family member was available to help.

When the doorbell rang she hurried to open.

"I'm Marco," said the Ambulance man.

They helped Alec into the lift but as it started, the patient slumped unconscious. Marco caught him. At the ground floor Florrie jammed her suitcase to keep the lift doors open. They could see the ambulance through the building's glass entrance.

"Please tell the driver to bring a stretcher," said Marco.

It was too late for the sad news to reach us so we bounced along without the least idea that my father was dying in Mallorca. When we did at last learn of his illness our trip became a race against death.

****

That nappy bucket was a most useful device. As we reached Mbeya (Tanzania) the prototype burst, spewing water and diapers liberally. Thinking of the mess, you may find it hard to believe that the explosion was incredibly lucky. But had it happened any further along on our journey we would never have been able to replace the pail. However, in Mbeya we found a splendid, huge and strong, plastic bucket. As I carried it back to Pythagoras I met a Belgium émigrée from the Congo.

'Madame' pointed in amazement at the container.

"*Mais*! Vat vill you vant viv zat?"

"It's an essential part of our equipment. Inside it will be water containing a dose of Napisan – that's stuff that cleans and sterilises nappies."

"Oh!" said Madame rather uncertainly but obviously doing her best to follow my strange ideas.

"Placed on the floor in front of the passenger seat the bucket

and its contents will be warmed by the car's transmission. Jolted about all day it works as a very fine washing machine."
"Ah! *Quelle bonne idée!* (What a brilliant idea!)". Madame now appreciated the details. "So every evening you have only to rinse the nappies. You will drape them about *inside* the tent, I hope, because of Putsi Flies."

Those nasty little insects lay their eggs in damp material. When the dried washing is then worn, maggots hatch from the eggs and penetrate the wearer's flesh, which becomes painfully infected and swollen. Either washing has to be dried indoors – free of the flies – or the eggs must be killed by ironing.
"But of course," I agreed, adding: "We actually keep everything inside because on previous trips we've learnt that garments and tea towels left overnight to dry on guy ropes are often eaten by wandering animals with depraved tastes. Saucepans, empty tins, etc. get carried off by hungry 2- or 4- footed visitors."

"O! *Quel horreur*!" exclaimed the good lady throwing up her hands and shaking her head. "You are surely *dérangée* (mad) to make this *voyage.*"

Grinning at her reactions, and wanting to shock her further, I showed her how a plastic basin, weighted down with impedimenta that would be needed during the day, fitted tightly inside the top of the bucket and stopped water from sloshing out.
"And see this 4-litre plastic bottle leaning against the transmission here – near the pail – It's full of clean water. Like the nappy bucket, it gains heat through the day. By evening the water's always at just the right temperature for Bruce's bath in the little basin that the top of the bucket holds so firmly."
"Heavens! – You put your son into *that*? Does he not fall out?"
"Bruce enjoys being dunked into the warm water, and the convenient height makes bath time easier for me."
"O!" gasped Madame again. "Surely you do not bath the baby *al fresco*? – Impossible!"
She recovered enough to ask:
"Is it true that you propose to pass by Land Rover across Zaire?"

"Yes."
The lady, recently escaped from that dread country where she'd spent many years, felt she knew it very well. She tapped her forehead.
"And with the Bébé?"
"Yes." The tapping became more frantic.
"Of a surety you should consult a brain specialist," she advised me seriously.
Later her husband, adding dire predictions of what we would meet ahead, agreed emphatically. We shut our ears.

8. Tubbing Bruce at the very end of *The Daftest Journey.*

CHAPTER FOUR

Reaching Zaire via the Ruzizi Delta

(Ruzizi can also be spelled as Rufifi or Rusisi.)

The émigrés lugubrious advice didn't deter us. We pushed on through Tanzania and into Burundi. Then, to get from Bujumbura, the capital of Burundi, into Zaire we had to cross a huge uninhabited delta where the Ruzizi River spills into the north of Lake Tanganyika. In that squelching region a serial killer was reliably reputed to have dispatched hundreds of locals and presumed to have eaten them. We kept a good look out for him among the bulrushes.

Unfortunately we missed Gustave – the evil 6 metre long crocodile. A pity! I wanted a picture. Bob, on the other hand, was glad. He had visions of me creeping through papyrus to get a close-up, and ending in Gustave's 451st scaly embrace.

An isolated, decrepit cabin revealed Burundi's exit border. Beyond that, empty No-Man's Land stretched as far as the eye could see: just quagmire with a broken causeway carrying a rotted, collapsing, mud track. Many square miles of rushes, sedges and other water plants surrounded us. Terribly far away were mauve mountains, dwarfed by distance – nothing else. This depressing morass had been a constant war zone for seven recent years, with battles raging forwards and back. A nightmare prospect fit to give anyone gooseflesh.

I whispered as if afraid to raise ghosts:

"Think of all those hundreds of exhausted men, in various stages of torn camouflage, dragging themselves painfully along these stinking canals and desperately grappling hand to hand across such vast areas of ooze – spearing, shooting, stabbing each other, tearing out each other's entrails... Anyway – what did those wretched, terrified soldiers understand about the aims of such vicious conflicts, that they were being forced to fight?"

Bob gazed round with a shiver. We didn't know that soon the place would again become the scene of bloody combat.

At each of the numerous streams we stopped and usually had to devise a method to cross. 'Sort-of' bridges sometimes existed; but even then poles had to be lugged about to strengthen the shaky span. During our civil engineering undertakings water birds rustled through reeds, squawking now and again as they splashed and dived for fish and frogs.

Eventually, insignificant in all the empty wasteland, we beheld, a battered, prefabricated hovel made of sheets of iron. It wavered at a crazy angle like a loose tooth. More than half of it drooped over the edge of a shallow ravine that had been gouged out of the silt by gales and flowing water. The sagging rear section was propped a couple of metres above the fearsome bog on piles of stones and by poles that looked more optimistic than effective. The floor of the back half of the hut had long since given place to a gaping hole. Without windows, light trickled in through the blank doorway, and via countless gaps in tattered roof and walls. I was so shocked that I couldn't stop myself. Like an umbrella-flourishing tour guide I announced, as if to an audience of holidaymakers:

"The tiny, teetering, tin hut tottering before you is the Immigration and Customs control for Zaire – the second largest country in Africa!"

(These days, after the division of The Sudan, it's probably *the* biggest country in Africa – and that's saying something in that continent of superlatives.)

"Careful!" exclaimed Bob in horrified tones. "Don't let them hear you disparage anything."

He was jittery because the previous day in Bujumbura I'd been arrested for snapping a pic of a memorial arch. The camera had almost been confiscated and I'd only *just* wriggled free. You'd think they'd be pleased to have their monuments shown to the rest of the world. But no – I was taken for a spy! Spying *what?*

The gloomy interior of that shocking portal to a colossal country contained just one cheap table and two men dosing uncomfortably on rickety chairs. There was no unpleasantness, only total incompetence. As at many other border posts, to obtain vital documents we had to exert huge quantities of patience and induce the bewildered guards to let us complete vehicle *carnet* and personal forms ourselves. The almost illiterate officials then raised problems before they stamped the page.

Usually the number and viciousness of the difficulties they invented depended upon the state of their digestions, how much they had over-imbibed, how many drugs they had taken and whether or not they had enjoyed a siesta.

9. Entry post into Zaire. (It did not, in fact, have windows.) For fear of being arrested we didn't dare take a photo so a sketch must suffice.

The truly amazing details of that day are reported in *The Daftest Journey* but since they happened *before* we got into Zaire and this book is about *crossing* that country I won't describe them here. I'll just say that having now entered Zaire, we later had to pass briefly into and then out of Rwanda.

Negotiating through so many (6 to be precise) stressful frontiers in such close proximity put us on edge, especially as the final border post back into Zaire was absolutely packed with yelling people. It was a mystery why this shack was so busy when elsewhere there had been neither people nor traffic. We got shoved forwards because, luckily, Bruce intrigued the locals, especially as he chose this moment to demand sustenance and wasn't going to be denied his routine even if we *were* surrounded by a horde of smelly, vociferous fellow travellers! Giving joyous cries, clapping and stamping, the crowd exclaimed over the fact that white infants drew succour in the same way as their own, and pawed at the baby.

Inside the inadequate shed bodies sweating from heat and tenseness thronged tightly all round, everyone clamouring for attention. Voices were raised. Outside, Pythagoras was left for once unguarded because as far as bureaucrats were concerned, Bob, being the man, and therefore the only member of our group who counted, had to deal with officials; and I was also needed in the hut (as a mere interpreter). Hence we had to keep one eye on the vehicle, another on our pockets and documents, and an extra eye on the compilation of paperwork. It would have been handy if we'd had chameleon eyes!
We were tense when, for the only time on the entire trip, our International Health Booklets were demanded. Luckily the officials examined them upside down. (No, really! – It's true, not a hackneyed joke!) They also sought our Smallpox and Yellow Fever certificates on the wrong pages of the little blue folders. We breathed again when no one noticed that mine had been issued in *Southern Rhodesia.* (Actually *Southern* Rhodesia had been acceptable by Black Africa, but when it turned into independent *Rhodesia* it became anathema to countries further north). That small, vital 'Southern' detail might not have been understood.

After a *very long* time and a few more bizarre delays, we were allowed to leave the heaving hell. But this time the pen-pusher had aspired to literacy and had not allowed us to do the paperwork ourselves. Ten days later his mistakes landed us in a mind-boggling near-disaster.

CHAPTER FIVE

Bukavu: Underground dinner. Warrior ants.

Distance means nothing. Between the first and last control posts in that infernal swamp were fewer than 90 miles, but the track was so ghastly that leaving Bujumbura at about 09.30, we didn't reach Bukavu till shortly before dusk, without stopping for lunch. There we met a tall Englishman called Edward who, although still relatively young, was stooped and grey-haired. Happy to meet compatriots, he very kindly invited us to stay the night in the house that he shared with three fellow teachers.

"Place yourselves into my car. I will make you a tour," he said. (Having lived in the region so long he now had difficulty speaking his mother tongue.)

"Bukavu was, in past times, a *magnifique* resort. All people called it '*La Perle du Congo'.* (The Pearl of the Congo.)"

Through red and gold glories of impending sunset our host took us on a distressing circuit. Ruins stretched over ridges and valleys of five gorgeous promontories, called 'the green hand', that dipped its 'fingers' into beautiful Lake Kivu.

"Bukavu, was in the sixties three times destroyed," said Edward, his sad face matching a lifeless tone.

"The last and greatest destruction occurred in 1967, when the so notorious Schramme and his mercenaries were besieged here."

Tactlessly Bob remarked:

"It doesn't look as if any effort has been made to re-build."

"Very few Europeans – for example, I – remained here throughout poor Bukavu's travails and I can avow you that not a morsel of rehabilitation (he meant 'no scrap of reconstruction') has been achieved since many years before Schramme was here. I myself was left with nothing. Only clothes for my back.

My friends, most were killed; some fled. Since 1967 my wife resides in England undergoing the medical treatment."

The hilly roads were indescribably bad. We were shocked to see numerous once-thriving, industrial sites infested with huge weeds, and couldn't understand why our host wanted to show us such dereliction. Maybe inflicting upon visitors the desecration of his erstwhile lovely city, now raped and razed, helped Edward to purge his trauma. Having survived through earlier battles over the city, he had finally been forced to watch the burning of his home and all his possessions including a tea/coffee estate then worth £250,000 – an immense sum in those days. Previously a fabulously rich man with a retinue of servants and workers, now in late 1971, more or less a pauper, he taught at a local Mission School. I hoped that he didn't teach English! His story was just one of many similar histories.

Wondering why he stayed, we gazed, aghast, at gaunt, blistered walls where only bleak corners remained insecurely poking up amid crumbling debris. Burnt and roofless homes, destroyed shops and former offices were just eyeless shells. The entire place seemed like the remains of a mouldering mouth full of vast, black, decayed teeth.

In contrast, proud, elegant and unscathed, Bukavu Cathedral's modern dome stood isolated on a separate hill – testimony to the Almighty's protection? – or to local superstitious beliefs? However, the adjacent horrifying shantytown held more destitute, displaced people in utter squalor than the entire population of Blantyre (the thrumming commercial capital of Malawi that was our home). Bukavu was undoubtedly grim and the next day we left it depressed; but afterwards we realized that in its dismal ruins there probably lurked more semblance of commerce and life than remained in the rest of the collapsed country.

We invited our 4 hosts to dinner. They suggested a crepuscular restaurant which seemed to be skulking away from Authority in a cellar that was reached via horribly narrow steps.

"Make attention to the stairway," said Edward. "It's *précipiteux* and *totalement sans illumination*." (Steep and dark.)

10. Bukavu Cathedral.

"However does the proprietor manage to get such good quality stuff?" I asked as I munched a delicious steak. "This meal is really excellent!"
Nobly Bob refrained from adding:
"And it's horrendously expensive'!"
"Oh, we have no trouble obtaining anything — so long as we pay. Nameless aeroplanes, entirely painted black, arrive regularly from 'the unmentionable country'. (South Africa)"
To hide labels flaunting its origins, our wine was presented in a cloak-and-dagger manner.

"My friends would like to settle the bill using Traveller's Cheques," Edward told the restaurateur. "And since tomorrow is Sunday, when the bank will be closed, they'd like to cash some extra money. Can you manage that?"
"*Pas de problème*," smiled the Belgian proprietor, adding: "In view of where they're hoping to go they'd better change a lot. They won't find banks along the way."
Since he charged a shocking commission it was not surprising that he looked happy.

Needless to say no telephones were working so I was anxious about how Brother Guillaume, a friend of the family, was coping with 5 children whom he had agreed to babysit in return for a pack of patience cards and unlimited supplies of whisky. I needn't have worried. It wasn't necessary for the good Brother to summon us by pedalling his creaky bicycle through desperately dark and deeply rutted alleys, braving thugs who would kill for his spectacles or to grab his jacket. That night 7-week-old Bruce distinguished himself by sleeping from 7.30pm till 5.30am – a clear demonstration of the exhaustion that overtook us all after the extraordinary Bujumbura-Bukavu crossing – or did the priest serve him a slug of Vat 69?

The unexpectedly civilised, multilingual and sometimes uproarious evening was only marred by more horrendous stories about *Le Grand Trou* – (The Big Hole – an infamous pothole ahead of us). We had first heard about that notorious hazard from a Malawian petrol server and then from border officials when we entered Tanzania several days ago; and the emigrés in Mbeya had also horrified us with its description. So had a priest in a remote village of Tanzania. The obstacle had to be awful to justify such widespread stories and the tales were becoming increasingly lurid as the distance to the terror lessened.

It was hard to visualise a vast continuous pothole 3 metres deep and 1 kilometre long but we were assured that gradually worn out by the passage of juggernauts through rocks and deep mud, it had become so terrible that it was now totally impassable. Each time we heard about it the obstacle seemed to increase in venom. Now it was again discussed with bated breaths; so we returned 'home' at 1am wondering what we were about to encounter in the days to come.

At Edward's house we found chaos. No, it wasn't the children who had driven the priest distracted. They were still sleeping like cherubs; but in a state of panic, Brother Guillaume and a couple of servants were sweeping the ground with eucalyptus switches.

"Driver Ants!" they panted. "They're marching right across the garden! See, we're doing our best but they're still scrambling forwards."

My blood froze! Each tiny, voracious creature in the menacing horde was incredibly light yet as many squirming millions poured forwards in a long, straight murderous stream we heard dry leaves crackling under their combined movement. *"Mon Dieu!"* screamed our hostess. "Millions of them... Advancing through our vegetables! Warn the neighbours! That black plague never turns aside."

The chickens must have squawked and fluttered about in their hut but many weren't heard in time. They could escape through a gap near the top of the poultry house and if the pea-brained creatures remembered the hole, it worked well – except for occasions when Genet cats discovered the opening and enjoyed a feast. Most of the birds, still muttering and fidgeting fearfully, were now roosting uneasily in nearby trees – but in the torchlight bones picked completely clean and pathetic feathers showed what had become of less enterprising fowl, that had not scrambled out. We arrived too late for one wretched hen which had stayed in her ground-level nest to protect chicks. There was nothing left of the babies and the brave mother, although still alive and still desperately pecking randomly in all directions, was in such a deplorable state that she had to be put out of misery.

Reports claim that Warrior Ants (also known as Army Ants and Driver Ants) first attack nostrils, filling them with their bodies to suffocate their prey before tearing off flesh, but when I lived in Ethiopia it seemed that the terrifying pests went straight for eyes. If we didn't reach our turkeys in time we would have to destroy still-living birds that had empty, bleeding eye sockets; and in the stables the ants tackled hoofs and stung their ways up legs of terrified, stamping and whinnying horses.

It is said that when he heard of approaching Army Ants, Dr Schweitzer (in Lambaréné) used to rush out to his chicken house, fling open the doors and force the birds to fly out.

During the convivial evening before the Ants drama, we

learnt that our most direct route to Kisangani was definitely closed. The jungle had taken over. An alternative, going through Goma, was sometimes passable if not recently subjected to rain.
"It's the only route," said the restaurateur with conviction.
"But '*Le Grand Trou'!* It will *sûrement* block your way."

11. Genet: "Chicken for supper? Can I squeeze in?"

CHAPTER SIX

Lake Kivu. 04.30 Military Approach

Edward oozed worry as we prepared to leave Bukavu the next morning.

"Where will you sleep?"

"We usually prefer to pitch our tent in the bush. Wild animals don't hurt, but in villages there are usually thieves."

"Yes. *C'est exact.* Yet Zaire is different. Wild war-men inhabit even in the densest forest. I ask you – I, who am speaking to you," in his anguish Edwards became very Gallic. "I implore you. In this country there is danger. It is occluded – all round. I myself, I know it. Seek if you can find a mission that has not been burnt to the ground. Ask to build your tent within their compound – if it exists still. Or hope that you might locate a friendly hamlet."

Thanking our kind host we set off with grim expressions. "Now," said Bob, "we're really faced with unknown territory plus problematic conditions."

"Yes. And we've had it really drummed into us that it will all be awful," I agreed.

Suddenly our bubble of optimism seemed to flicker and, although it didn't quite burst, it certainly wasn't as robust as it had been. Having always assumed that we'd get through to Europe, now we began to wonder.

Although we realised it would not be in good condition, we had hoped to take what was shown on the map as an excellent, direct thoroughfare right across Zaire heading north***west*** from Bukavu. But the jungle had swallowed all the erstwhile wonderful highways so not even remnants of that existed. Instead we had to head ***east* of north** along the only track available and we did not see even a vestige of what had once been the good artery branching off to our left. Compulsory, appreciable deviations of that sort marked our progress all the way through the D.C.R. Juddering on, we had to choose our route according to which trails might perhaps be passable. As a result we progressed along many small zigzags and achieved *overall* a vast jagged trajectory shaped like this:

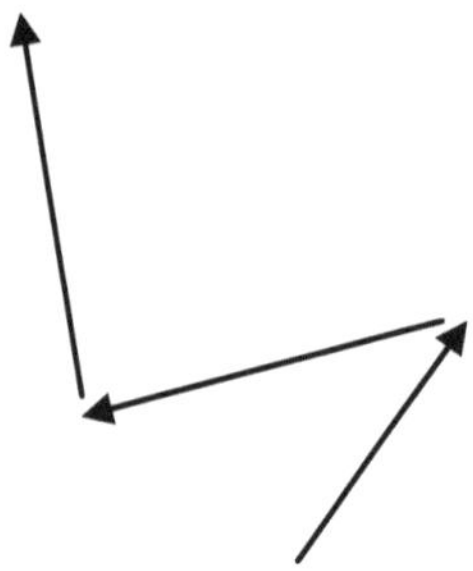

(Hundreds of small zigzags are not shown.)

When, on slithery mud, we left Bukavu and began our drive through the war-ravaged country we had no premonition of the enormous, exhausting crisscross ahead, or that we were about to wade deep through adventure.

Did we know that our route cut through the world's biggest Rain Forest after the Amazon? I don't think so. Anyway, if that had put us off, there was no other itinerary – except via the Sudan where conflicts were, as usual, in full swing. So we skidded hopefully away from the wreck of what had been The Pearl of the Congo. Constant concentration while skating around in potholed Congolese sludge became a 'given' until, 10 days later, we left Zaire – with lots of fabulous memories, but no regrets whatsoever!

We progressed from Bukavu to Goma, Beni, Buna... the list of places we passed through will be familiar to anyone who has followed the news. They have been sites of horrendous atrocities and blood-curdling massacres, repeated again and again both in the years before we travelled and subsequently. We caught a rare more-or-less battle-free moment.

Rampant media publicity has for decades covered the continued fighting and dreadful devastation in this region. On television stunningly-beautiful hills and plains have swarmed with shattered refugees who hump babies and pathetically inadequate bundles of scant possessions to escape vicious guerrillas. They aim for shelter only to have to move on – or often, simply forced to return to the demolished villages that they had previously evacuated. It is hard for us to imagine what misery it must be to live through such agonies.

Leaving Bukavu we climbed, sometimes reaching 2,138m, delighted by the chance to look round and absorb the wonderful mountain scenery. I found extra covering for Bruce and buttoned my sweater. Then my eyes turned to Lake Kivu very far below.

"Look – dozens of little islands. How lovely!" I exclaimed.

"D'you know that Lake Kivu contains the world's tenth largest inland island?"

"Well, I do now. – What on earth's an 'inland island', anyway'?"

"An island in an inland sea, of course. Lots of the Rift Valley lakes are so huge that they are inland seas."

"An island in an inland sea!" I repeated thinking that there was no 'of course' about it at all. "What a strange concept!"

22. Pythagoras leaves Bukavu, showing his BC 585 number, the sand tracks and the rubber bag made from an inner tube that contained truly *vital* items. Lake Kivu with a small 'inland island' is in the background.

Green 'inland islands' (!) were set in sparkling, cyan-coloured water with patches of emphatic cobalt shadows. All round soft-sided mountains rose in blue and smoky grey folds. It was a magnificent, innocent-looking sight that belied deadly chemistry.

Blantyre people may have thought us mad but they had lent us tomes, ancient and recent, relevant to our journey. Using those books we had prepared notes. Out loud for Bob's benefit, I now had a conversation with our loose-leaf notebook.

Book: '*Like other parts of the Rift Valley Lake Kivu is of volcanic origin*.'

Me: "Well – of course – everyone knows that!"

'*This 18th largest lake in the world is breathtakingly beautiful*'–

"Yes, O.K., Book, we can see the beauty for ourselves. Hm, 18th largest... That's saying a lot. But Lake Malawi, you know, where we live, is the 10th largest in the world. "

'*Kivu has the great depth of 480 m*'

(Sarcastically:) "Oh, really! Well, Lake Malawi is the deepest: 706 m deep – so snooks to Kivu then!"

Bob didn't let me get away with being so rude. On Kivu's behalf he put in:

"Kivu lies at the highest spot within the Rift Valley."

"You shouldn't be so knowledgeable!"

I sought another point for Malawi. "Well – Lake Malawi – er – ... Oh yes! – It's at the very southernmost end of the Great Rift – and at its lowest section, only 50m above sea level.

"The variation's amazing, isn't it – how the Rift Valley's full of hills and valleys and volcanoes...? I always imagined the bottom of the Rift Valley to be a horizontal plain, between cliffs."

"And both lakes have a fascinating history and incredible wild life, outside and within the water," finished my husband as if he was clinching a hugely important matter. I interrupted.

"But listen to this:

'*Lake Kivu has sinister, attributes because it is one of only three known volumes of water world-wide that, from time to time explode and provoke violent upsets of the lake's layers*.'

Daphne: "How can water 'explode'?"
Bob: "If you read on I expect the notes will tell you."
So I continued reading aloud:
'There is evidence that over aeons this gigantic natural reservoir has upended itself several times and it will be catastrophic when Kivu again, inevitably, suddenly froths up like a shaken bottle of fizzy drink.'

(An example of such an outburst occurred in The Cameroons in 1986 when Lake Nyos, much smaller than Kivu, exploded with tragic results. Luckily Lake Nyos remained calm in 1971 when we crossed The Cameroons.)

"I don't remember writing that guff," remarked Bob.
"Naturally you don't. *You* didn't put it into our notebook. *Dai* did. He's a geologist. Remember? Listen!
'Carbon dioxide, which accumulates in the lake from volcanic leaks, is converted by microbes in the water into methane. CO_2 suffocates and methane is combustible.
"How charming!" muttered Bob sardonically. "So presumably the methane explodes. I suppose that's why they say the water turns over. After that the carbon dioxide suffocates anything that's alive. Did you find out why all this melodrama happens and why?"
I turned back to the book.
'At the top of Lake Kivu are 63m of water containing oxygen. Below that lie distinct layers of water. They don't mix – like oil and vinegar in a salad dressing. These permanently stratified lower layers contain no O_2. Each of them is itself homogenous and stable, and each has its own mixture of the two dangerous gases, CO_2 and methane, at various pressures.'
"There's a diagram," I added.
"I'll look at it when we change drivers."
"If volcanic sparks are produced or unusual heating is created , for example by movement of the magma under the lake, the methane will explode.
"Heavens! Why didn't you tell me about this before?"

"Could we have missed Lake Kivu in order to avoid the possible eruption?"
"No. You know perfectly well that our course is the only possible way at the moment. Everywhere else is messed up by local wars."

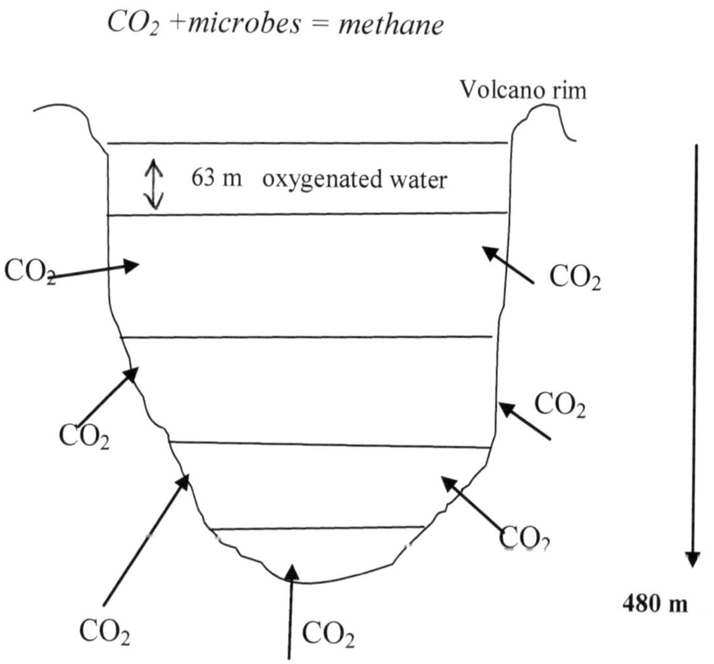

12. Lake Kivu cross section. (Not to scale.)

'The explosion will cause a tsunami. In a nutshell the event will consist of the following steps: A great expanse of territory round the lake will be: first incinerated by burning methane exploding like an atomic mushroom, then crushed by monstrous waves, and finally smothered as CO_2 creeps heavily from the lake stifling all surrounding life for a immense area.

"Good grief! I hope it doesn't happen right now!"
Bob looked round as if expecting a gigantic wave to appear. In

fact he was hunting for the dam that was built in 1958 to control the Ruzizi River as it flows out of Lake Kivu and forms the delta – where Gustave lived.

"Judging by our squelching journey from Bujumbura the dam doesn't seem to be achieving much!" he concluded.

Instead of smashed hydroelectric generators we spotted couple of Sacred Ibis stalking solemnly along the lake's edge with their black heads cocked and long curved beaks (equally black) ready to plunge at food. Large and white, their bodies showed up clearly against dark vegetation as they studied the possibility of a tasty frog or a wriggling fish.

13. Sacred Ibis.

Stunning (and huge) Lake Kivu was to our east (right) all the way to Goma but we lost sight of it as we dropped from its magnificent surrounding mountains to a volcanic plain at 916m.

(For comparison: Top of: Ben Nevis: 1,344m; Mont Blanc, highest mountain in Western Europe: 4,810m; Kilimanjaro: 5,895m.)

Like the birds we ignored Kivu's deadly aspects, and laboured on still heading northeast up the Great Rift Valley, and away from East Africa's open savannah towards moist equatorial forest.

One night, within a cramped clearing that was squashed all round by forest, there was a tiny wooden church with a mere handful of homes, and just enough space for our tent on the damp ground between two little mud huts whose palm leaf roofs hung down almost to the black soil. We slept soundly till the most incongruous of sounds shocked us awake at 04.30.
"Daphne!" gasped Bob tremulously. "Are you awake!"
"Yes." My whisper was just as frightened.
"Do you know what it is?"
"Well – a band of some sorts." I didn't want to expand on uncomfortable thoughts that were thudding through my head.
"But it's pitch black."
Pause.
Bob again:
"Do you realise what they're playing?"
I replied shortly, so as not to give away my worries.
"Yes. *Marche Militaire*."
"Are they coming to attack us?"
"Don't know. They're awfully close."
"Have you got the hammer?"
Yes. It's in my hand. Have you got the machete?"
"Yes."
We always had these implements beside our bedrolls every night, but they didn't afford much comfort.
"Whoever they are they're bound to be much bigger and heaps stronger than we are. We'll never hold our own against any attackers."
"Yes. D'you know how many thousands of whites have been massacred in the Congo in recent years?"

"No. And don't tell me."

There was nothing more to say. We'd put up a gigantic fight but...

Was our undefended tent about to be hacked to pieces? Were we going to add to the countless whites who had been butchered in recent years? Not knowing how to cope, we slipped out of sleeping bags and crouched on them, sweating from horror but frozen with fright, knowing that, despite the machete and enormous hammer we'd stand absolutely no chance. Utterly awful, through misty drizzle the dreadful beat of *Marche Militaire* played on cornets and trumpets approached, sounding terrifyingly *'militaire'.*

There was a pause. Deep voices rumbled from beside the neighbouring hut. Were they deciding upon an attack strategy?

Then we heard "Auld Lang Syne"!

"Good grief!" breathed Bob. "I don't believe it!"

I was too stunned to speak. What was about to happen?

The music stopped. The sound of footsteps clattered away through trees.

It took us some time to relax, and to our shame, we didn't emerge into the murky pre-dawn to applaud the players. At 6.00 while we were in the midst of packing the sodden tent, the entire mission band, 5 chaps unusually spruce in long trousers and clean shirts, presented themselves for inspection.

"Was it you playing so brilliantly, early this morning?" we asked, tactfully avoiding any mention of the petrified panic they had induced.

"Yes. Yes. Did you like it?"

"Of course. It was superb," we lied.

Broad white grins showed their joy.

"How elegant you are!"

They preened with delight.

"May we take your photo?"

"Yes! Yes!"

"Of course!"

"Please take it!"

Beaming and thrilled to be snapped they posed this way and that, exploding with many cheerful comments.
"What is your address? We will send copies."
"Yes!"
Yes! We want copies"
"Take these eggs and rice," the bandsmen offered.
"Many thanks – but no."
"Please take them."
"You are very kind, but no! We do not need them. You must enjoy them yourselves."

Suddenly a furious bandmaster appeared and the atmosphere changed abruptly. We avoided a nasty scene only by assuring him that we would not be selling or showing their photos in Kinshasa or elsewhere.
"Other members of the mission have been so pleasant. Let's give the usual donation and escape as quickly as possible," I suggested.

Under the malevolent eyes of the still fulminating bandmaster, and the sad looks of our friends, we abandoned our customary careful packing, bundled the horribly wet gear higgeldy piggeldy into Pythagoras and cleared out. Later, surrounded by overwhelming, dripping branches, we found a spot by the roadside to breakfast, tidy up, and recover.

14. Zairian children in a more evolved village.

CHAPTER SEVEN

Overgrown crops. Giant gnat.

Thoughts about LGT. Cries in neighbouring hut.

As we travelled north from Lake Kivu impressive volcanoes sprinkled the plain to our left. They have since changed shape by erupting, but they remain awesome. To our right, rearing against the sky, a continuous line of other potential exploders formed the bulky border with Rwanda and Uganda. (The year before we had walked at great altitudes on slopes of those volcanoes looking for and at gorillas. There were no gorilla parks in those days so the creatures we watched were still very wild.)

During the first half of the 20th century, this eastern region of the Congo that we were now crossing was part of the 'private domain' of King Leopold of Belgium. Here the jungle was cleared and replaced with vast properties whose tea/coffee/quinine provided great wealth for the royal purse.

In the sixties war devastated homes, villages, most infrastructure and agriculture so, by 1971, abandoned tea bushes, normally trimmed to neat low heights for easy plucking, loomed above us unbelievably ten metres high and shockingly unkempt. Coffee was sprouting extravagantly, pushing upwards in unregulated profusion; and even more enormous, untended quinine trees demonstrated the desperate degeneration of the once-flourishing area.

Blank-faced idlers, who in years past had been employed on efficient estates, albeit under terrible conditions, now had no work. Even if any memory of how to survive off the wild jungle remained, that knowledge was useless because the giant trees had been removed. The locals therefore had nothing to do, no wages with which to buy essentials and no forest in which to forage, yet they seemed to lack any desire to scratch even a precarious living from the fertile soil. They loitered beside the road throwing stones at vehicles that passed only rarely. Luckily they were bad shots so Pythagoras was only scratched.

Pointing to the overgrown vegetation I urged:
"These huge feral trees that should all be nicely-shaped, productive bushes give me claustrophobia. Let's find a gap where we can have lunch with at least some sort of view, and where there aren't hordes of loafers."

16. Malawian tea picker. Bushes are kept low for easy plucking. The oilskin coat protects against snakes and spiders as well as the weather.

Throughout the trip lunches were always cold snacks by the roadside. While we ate, Bruce relaxed, usually naked and happy, on a baby-sized sheet that I spread over the big plastic bag holding clean nappies. This soft 'mattress' lay on dust/grit/grass/mud beside the picnic case that contained all our nutritive needs for the day. We watched unremittingly to ensure that no mosquito (or worse) took a fancy to the baby's blood.

This time *Bruce* escaped; but as I handed my husband the box of salad (carefully washed in potassium permanganate solution to kill germs), I noticed a couple of 'small helicopters'.
"Heavens! Look at those colossal wasps!"
"More like gi-normous gnats," responded Bob, helping himself

from the tin of ham. "Splendid clipped-in waists," he added admiringly. "They're almost not there. How does their food get past that constriction?"
"Mustard? Amazing wings! Such a huge span – and glorious rainbow colours."

Suddenly, without any provocation, one of the magnificent creatures made a beeline towards Bob's nose. It hovered for a split second and he tried to swipe it away.
"OUCH!" he yelled at the top of his voice, leaping into the air. "The brute's stung me!"
Immediately his upper lip and nostril started to swell. The attacker did not leave an embedded sting so I rushed to our medicine tin for anti-bite cream and anti-histamine tablets.

"The blighter!" The sufferer complained bitterly, holding his face as he marched, staccato fashion, backwards and forwards along the road. "Oh my goodness! Crickey! Ow! It's *agony*!"

Although painful for several days the spectacular swelling gradually reduced and eventually all traces disappeared. We continued to express astonishment but, once it became obvious that no serious harm had been done, we couldn't help laughing.
"Cheeky devil! Fancy zooming in without any 'by your leave' or 'if you please'!"
"It probably thought your nose was an ideal dark hole in which to make a nest," I teased.
"But the wretch was far too big to get even its head inside my nostril!"
"Yes. But if you'd only left the horrendous thing alone you'd have had the privilege of lots of little mud balls stuffed in to make an elegant egg container, then a horde of little gnats – or hornets – or whatevers – eventually emerging from it!"
"Thanks very much!" said Bob bitterly. "You forgot about caterpillars pushed in to feed the little ones when they hatched! How did you know it'd always been my ambition to brood a clutch of monsters in my nose?"

That evening a small crowd watched and threw questions as we pitched the tent. One onlooker, who professed to drive a beer lorry, gasped when he heard we were planning to go ahead along the only available route - via *Le Gran Trou*. (LGT)

17. The 'men' at lunch. Bob swats an insect.

"I just operate here, in the Eastern Region," he assured us. "I would *never* try to enter the rest of Zaire – (i.e. beyond *LGT).*"
"That will undoubtedly stop you," added his pal gleefully, and proceeded to regale us with more blood-freezing details of the outsized pothole. "Even huge trucks can't get through."

Over supper Bob reminded me
"If we can't beat the tremendous obstacle we'll have to back-track a day's journey to turn into Uganda. Then, with luck, we'll manage a huge loop through East Africa, before attempting to re-enter Zaire many miles to the north.
"So we have to face the monster pothole because we're arriving from the south," I concluded. "If we'd come from East Africa we could have skipped this section of Zaire?"
"Yup. But this region is new to us. We've 'done' East Africa lots of times."
Bob's constant studying of the map enabled him to add:
"The detour will cost us – if we have to do it – and if it exists – an extra 1,000 miles, a lot of time and money, and goodness knows how much wear and tear on Pythagoras and ourselves. I *really* don't want to do that circuit."
As the visa expert I voiced another concern.
"In the Ruzizi swamp we 'entered' Zaire twice. I wonder – does our multiple-entry visa extend to *three* admissions?"
"If a third entry into Congo is refused we'll have to crawl back home." Bob's voice was edgy.

There was only one option: we HAD to negotiate a way through LGT. Would we manage that? If not – which Club pessimist would win the wagers when we slunk back, tails between our legs?

I woke in the dark hours thinking that Bruce was yelling; but when I looked into the basket he was sleeping peacefully. The howls stopped. Next morning, just next to our tent, a woman sitting on the ground outside her primitive hut was nursing a baby. Like Bruce he was naked and plump.
"How old is your son?" I asked, tickling his toes.

"He is, I think, maybe about 52 days." The woman smiled proudly. "And your baby?"
I had to laugh; and using her idiom as I pointed to Bruce, I said: "This one – he is *exactly* 52 days old."
"Aa-i-ee!" squealed the woman in delight, and shouted to her friends who congregated, all cackling like chickens.

I realised that in the hut right up close to our tent a babe of precisely the same age as ours had woken, cried and been fed. Maybe it was naïve of the Africans to exclaim in amazement when they saw our white baby suckling just as their own infants did; but I was equally silly to be astonished by the precise similarity of the midnight cries to those emitted by a hungry Bruce.

Now the two infants were exactly on a par but their lives would differ radically. What might become of the mud hut baby? Famine? War? AIDS? Ebola? Bruce was placed in his Fish Basket and, leaving Goma, he continued his incredible journey across Africa.

44. Landing Eagle

CHAPTER EIGHT

Rapid lunch on the equator.

Bloody Schedule. Driving inside volcanoes.

Derelict pumps.

Nasty bump. Eyes glaring from dark jungle,

Today only death roams the Zairian plains that simmer in that part of the bottom of the Rift Valley. In 1971, although we shared the road with no other transport, there was abundant wild life. Lots of varied animals and birds, especially different types of splendid cranes, delighted us as we drove straight across an enormous, sweltering vastness: the Lake Albert National Park.

We were glad to climb away from scorching heat that was reflecting off caked mud. Rising from the expanse of black soil, the disintegrating gravel road seemed endless as we corkscrewed painfully up the Kabasha Escarpment from 3,000ft to 8,000ft.

"We've only done 100 miles in 41/2 hours," grumbled Bob.

"Don't moan! We're lucky that in this country, where maintenance is virtually unknown, the dreadful track's not so eroded that these tight hairpins are killers. And being forced to crawl has enabled us to appreciate the amazing views."

Bob growled at my determined cheeriness.

At the top there was a breath-taking panorama seen between vast podocarpus trees.

"How absolutely beautiful! Let's stop for lunch."

"What's that lake *way* down over there?"

"Where's the map? Er – Must be Lake Edward. We're just about right on the equator."

"I don't care where we are. I'm freezing! Let's exhume long trousers and sweaters."

"It'll be the first time Bruce has worn anything more than a nappy. He doesn't approve of clothes. He's wriggling like a kitten being dressed in a doll's outfit! Keep *still*, you little devil!"

Lunches tended to be rushed and this was a very typical meal. Details are recorded in our diaries so I am not inventing even one iota... I wrote:

"The view was grandiose, the immediate scenery wonderful with amazing vegetation, but our roof spider had finally lost its last leg so I spent the so-called 'rest' re-*roping* the equipment on top of Pythagoras, and supplying food to Bob who was (as usual) studying the map and his notes."

Not that scrutinising the map was necessary! There *was* only *one* route, but he seemed to derive consolation from trying to guess towards which compass point we could possibly soon be heading, and what progress we *might* manage – per*haps* – "If we're lucky!"

"Wouldn't it be fun if we had to pause at a splendid fork and wonder which Motorway to select," I teased. The answer was a grunt. Rattling our map impatiently the planner muttered:

"Sometimes the vegetation's so dense it's hard to believe that a way ahead actually *does* exist!"

And we hadn't yet reached the proper jungle!

Total lack of signposts didn't matter because such alternatives as presented themselves were simply whether or not a supposed road was worse than the deviation. We just experienced variations in conditions of the track: awful, ghastly, appalling and – (Surprise! Surprise!) – occasionally good.

After that particular lunch "break" of precisely 12.5 minutes I had the roof organised, picnic gear went back into the vehicle, and we were off. Then Bruce sucked while I munched what I had been able to grab. That was an extreme case, but the briefest of stops was normal. It was useless begging for a minute to snatch a photo or simply to enjoy a quiet moment. Bob invariably replied:

"We must Press ON. We're behind schedule" – which was a depressing pity. Bloody Schedule! My husband was scared we'd run out of money if we lingered. We didn't exactly have a great supply of filthy lucre.

'Bloody Schedule' became my silent mantra which I repeated never suspecting what was happening in Mallorca. If we'd known that my father was struggling for his very life we'd have rushed even more – and probably ended having an accident. My husband's flipping Schedule sat on our shoulders like a looming albatross gradually escaping our clutches. Eventually we reached Mallorca only a week 'late' but this was largely due to many days such as the one currently being described, en route for Beni, which turned out to be unpleasantly long and with only the very briefest lunch stop.

On my second turn of driving that day, the road actually curled *inside* some volcanoes. It's the most incredible experience to climb or drop on constricted roads going round and round *within* colossal cones. The interiors were lush and green, built up with tier after tier of amazing terraces cultivated by the local subsistence farmers. The enclosed volcano 'shelves' were a striking contrast to the enormous plains of the morning's Lake Albert National Park. I kept the steering wheel constantly at a slight angle to accommodate the unending bend.

"It must have been a helluva lot of work to make these narrow ledges!" remarked Bob fitting a new film into the cine.

"It exhausts me to think of the villagers labouring up and down so steeply to reach their tightly-curving fields," I agreed. "Their shoulder baskets and big hats... the pawpaw trees waving round their huts... It's all so picturesque, but I wonder what sort of mentality they develop with horizons bounded by the inside of a moderately small volcano."

Derelict petrol pumps were just one sign of the decay of past prosperity: sad testimony to the one-time richness, but current dereliction, of Kivu Province in particular, and of Zaire in general. Every crumbled service station increased our concern. Without fuel our trip would be as defunct as the burnt-out dispensaries, abandoned estates and ruined Missions that lined our route.

Threading a settlement after dark we found yet another broken pump. A loiterer suggested there *might* be supplies at Beni.

"What if that pump is devastated like this one, and the last three we've passed? How much beyond Beni can we go?"

"Doesn't make any difference. There's no fuel behind. We can't go back."

Reversing still-thirsty Pythagoras, Bob drove straight into the concrete plinth of the useless pump. CRASH! The Land Rover juddered and then shook off the trouble. The concrete didn't budge.

"Oh well. The only damage is a cut in my forehead. Serves me right," muttered my husband as I cleansed the gushing wound. With a plaster and his swollen lip he looked really murderous! Luckily without serious consequences, the silly accident nevertheless showed how tired we were.

Fate was not finished with us.

The night was fearsomely dark, and opaque as blancmange because of dense clouds. Suffocating walls of thick creeper-tangled trees pressed like a heavy old-fashioned eiderdown. We had not yet found anywhere safe to pitch the tent so, stiff and weary, we were rumbling on hoping that Beni would have a still-existing Mission. Pythagoras was full of silent tension as we longed to find somewhere to camp. The only positive thing about the moment was that the baby wasn't fractious. He had fallen into his usual deep sleep for the night.

A heavy thumping sounded the alarm. Bob shouted: "Stop!"

But he needn't have bothered because exclaiming "Puncture!" in disgusted tones I brought Pythagoras to a halt. On our entire journey – across the length of Africa and on to the north of Scotland, then back to Malawi – we had seven punctures – three of which occurred in Zaire. Suffering this one after dark was scary. You don't want to be immobilised anywhere in the Congo, and especially not at night.

"Thank God we've got the Hi-lift jack! The ground's so uneven here – the little official jack'd never manage."
"This wheel nut won't unscrew." Did I detect a note of panic?
With one hand I passed Bob our enormous hammer and pointed the torch (no head lamps in those days). In the other hand I held the nuts that had so far 'condescended' to come undone and be removed. (Never put them down. They'll vanish!)
"Gosh! It's really inky outside our tiny glimmer of light!"
My voice was muted with awe. There were tremors of fear running up and down my spine. Eerie rustles all round seemed to announce imminent danger.
"Hm!" Bob was intent on the extra-long-arm wheel spanner.
"I know now what 'impenetrable jungle' means."
"That's a cliché."
"Well – take a look round. I feel as if a thousand hidden eyes are glaring at us."
"Do you *have* to say such things?"
"Bob straightened up, glanced about, shivered and said:
"Er – yes."
He pulled himself together, unnecessarily hitched up his trousers, and added with unconvincing nonchalance:
"Well, let's get on with it then."

Surreptitiously looking over shoulders, we fitted the spare and trundled the punctured tyre towards Pythagoras's rear. In the torchlight we gazed at the damage with horror.
"Just look at that! The wall has simply collapsed, leaving huge ragged rips."
"So much for the extra-heavy-duty cross-country outer casings that we imported specially for the trip!" I said bitterly.
"They cost a bomb too!" exclaimed Bob furiously as together we lifted the heavy wheel into place. So far neither of us had regained enough strength to attempt such efforts alone.

Before leaving Blantyre, having loaded Pythagoras with goods, water, petrol, sand/mud tracks, and everything else that we would need – not forgetting Bruce and ourselves we went to the weighbridge to check that we had not exceeded the permitted weight. Despite this precaution the ghastly terrain was too much. The tyres could not take the pounding.

When the outer casing of a tyre collapsed the rim of the wheel hub inevitably smashed down onto the inner tube and ripped a huge rent in that. So whenever an 'outer' broke we had to repair that *and* a great tear in the inner tube as well.

"We'll have to strengthen this outer casing with gaiters."

('Gaiter' in this case refers to a piece of tough rubber glued to the inside of a tyre across a damaged region – liked a patch.)

"Whopping ones."

Disregarding exhaustion, punctures and depressing post-war wreckage, we generally plugged on happily enough in our mini world of the Land Rover. We acted as if we never realised that potential disaster could be imminent, yet Suppressed Tension was a permanent passenger.

What trouble would materialise round the next bend? What would the following day's 'road' be like? Would our planned route even *exist* tomorrow? As to the impending "*Grand Trou*" – we scarcely dared to mention that, but when I was feeding Bruce in the early hours, Bob started tossing and muttering desperately. He fought his sleeping bag as he tried to rotate his arms. He was obviously driving through some terrible obstacle.

"Stop dreaming about the LGT," I said as I shook his shoulder.

"Wha...?"

He turned over, gasped:

"Hey! It's terri – huge pit..." and went back to sleep!

Lucky fellow! Bruce sucked on; and in the unlit tent, listening to sounds of the African night, I wondered about what lay ahead and prayed desperately that the nightly downpours and daily light rain would stop.

CHAPTER NINE

Greek play. Fish Basket

Pythagoras finally struggled into Beni at 20.40 and squelched along the potholed, unpaved main-street. The only place to camp, perhaps safely, seemed to be the yard of the recently rebuilt Beni Hotel. The owner would have preferred us to increase his bank balance by using a room.
"Oh all right," he agreed in accented French, "but only if you dine here."
Good-naturedly he bullied his wife into providing a magnificent meal, which he served himself with hilarious actions and corny jokes. After we had bought him a drink he told us happily:

"Like so many Greek proprietors of local enterprises, I – Giorgio Papadopolos – have lived in eastern Zaire for 40 years."
Noticing that Bob was having difficulty with his French, versatile Giorgio swapped to English.

"In 1964 my hotel was flattened. I escaped to Kenya for 4 months to avoid being burnt alive. But I came back – of course!"
How could he say: 'of course'? We'd have been up and away forever after such experiences! His jocularity horrified and amused us.
"What's the weather been like recently?" Bob asked thinking ahead to terrifying LGT.
"Oh – not so bad. Very few showers..."
We breathed a little more easily.

Our host was the only person we ever met to treat the monster hole humorously.
"Of course it was three years ago that I passed there," he told us. "Since then *Le Grand Trou* usually makes the *only* east-west route across northern Zaire virtually impassable. Here in the Eastern Region we have been cut off from the rest of Zaire. But we can get things from Uganda, which these days enjoys more facilities than we have here."

In graphic display of how he had driven through LGT he raised his arms and twirled them violently clockwise and anticlockwise.
"See how I fought the steering wheel?"
To the detriment of his tubular dining-room chair he leapt energetically up and down showing us how the bumps had thrown him about. As he went on rotating his body and frantically threshing hairy arms he shouted:
"Look! It's like wrestling with a giant, writhing python."
All the time he bellowed a fearsome description of the 'mountainous' surface he was negotiating. In stitches we took it all with a large packet of salt; yet the next day we discovered that his antics had not been exaggerated!

As if sliced by a giant machete the yelling and gyrating suddenly stopped. Dead silence echoed round the big bare dining room with its metal furniture and tiled floor. We stared in horrified amazement at our host who was crouched on his seat nursing an elbow. On his face was a look of intense agony.
"What's..." cried Bob leaping from his seat. The chair's feet squealed as they scratched across the tiles.
I was shocked into immobility.
Kyria Papadopolos ran out from the kitchen wiping her hands on a tea towel.
"I assure you: in my struggles I broke my elbow against my car window," said the teasing Greek straightening up with a malicious grin. We breathed again!

The disturbing undertones to his description of *Le Grand Trou* suddenly had a frightening edge when, becoming serious, he added:
"You shouldn't take a baby that way. The jungle's so thick that not even the strongest or heaviest vehicle has ever attempted to smash a bypass through it to get round *Le Gran Trou*. And beyond that you're really in the uttermost wild.
"Lorry drivers wait in long queues for days, even weeks, sometimes months, until rain holds off. If the bottom of The Big Hole dries enough to become *perhaps* passable, then they try to shoot what has developed into a steep-walled canyon. They

often become bogged down, employ gangs of locals to dig and push, and, after several days of intense labour, if they don't remain permanently jammed till the next half-dry spell, they finally squelch out of the mire that lines the base of the 'gorge'."

"Awful!" muttered Bob. "In its wake each juggernaut must leave an even more pitted, rutted, and ruined surface."

"Of course."

The hotel manager nodded and went on macabrely:

"Sometimes those skidding, slithering monsters simply squash helpers against the gorge's jagged sides leaving dead or maimed bodies splattered along the rocky chasm."

Bob and I gasped. No wonder the disrepute of LGT had spread far and wide for literally hundreds of miles.

Wearing a Mediterranean-style wrap-right-round apron that proclaimed 'personally stitched' with every well-crafted seam, Mme P came to join us and directed a stream of machine-gun-like Greek at her spouse.

"I tell him stop his bad stories," she said, throwing aside her tea towel. "You tell us your trip. Yes?"

She was fascinated by Bruce's cradle so we launched into The Tale of the Fish Basket:

When the bombshell struck and we knew that, instead of two, we'd be three travellers we realised that, as well as varied safari paraphernalia, we'd have to carry gear for a tiny voyager whose luggage and size were in inverse proportions! The cradle would be the newcomer's largest bit of luggage.

Blantyre shops didn't sell baby items. A second-hand carrycot might have been available, but its sides would have been neither high enough to prevent the incumbent from being thrown out when (very frequently) we hit bumps and craters, nor tough enough to stop dislodged objects from landing on him.

"Oh." Mme P empathised sadly.

Malawians carried lake fish countrywide in marvellous woven-bamboo 'boxes' with strong and high walls. The Brat's crib, we decided, would be a large version of the common Malawian fish basket.

19. Basket stall in a Malawian market

This 'inspiration' was hard to achieve. Many varieties of woven-bamboo items were sold all over Malawi, yet nothing was suitable; and it seemed impossible to locate a weaver to make the cradle.

But one day our cook-houseboy arrived thrilled and grinning gleefully.

"Medem! My friend, he tell me one man can mebbe he make basket for bebby."

"Ah!" breathed Mme P with relief.

I became equally excited, but remained sceptical... Cook and I leapt into Pythagoras to follow footpaths,

stream banks and contradicting instructions till we reached a distant village.
"Can you make such as this?" I asked waving a drawing and a rough cardboard model of what was needed.
"Ndio, Medem!" nodded the weaver with a huge smile. ("Yes, Madam!")
Producing two sticks, I explained:
"Long like this big stick."
"Ndio, Medem!"
I indicated the width of my cardboard model, "Wide like this small stick."
"Ndio. Ndio!"

"He could make the basket?" asked our listeners.

"*Well – that's what he said... But did the grin simply mock our ideas? Was it produced only to keep me happy? Would he abscond with my advance payment? Negotiations apparently satisfactory, we went home and waited with mixed expectations.*

Weeks later Cook and I returned to the village fearing that there had not been enough water to soak the cane, or that the weaver was ill, or that he'd never returned from the funeral of his cousin's wife's uncle's sister-in-law... But our friend had made a beautiful creel with two semicircular arches as handles that would also support the mosquito net and divert flying objects.

I cut plastic foam to provide a shock-absorbent mattress and wall lining, and sewed covers for both – pale yellow – "

"Good for boy or girl," interjected Mme P knowledgably. "Myself I make always white. Put afterwards pink, blue ribbons."

We finished the Fish Basket Story:

"Here," said my neighbour, Anne. "Put this lace round the basket top. It's elasticised."
"Wow! Thanks! That does make it smart!" I exclaimed but flinched inwardly at the thought of how torn and filthy the pristine white lace would become on an arduous trans-African journey. I removed it as soon as we had left and wrapped it in a plastic bag."

Mme P thought that was an excellent idea. "You will put back when you reach to your home."
'*If* we ever get home,' I thought.

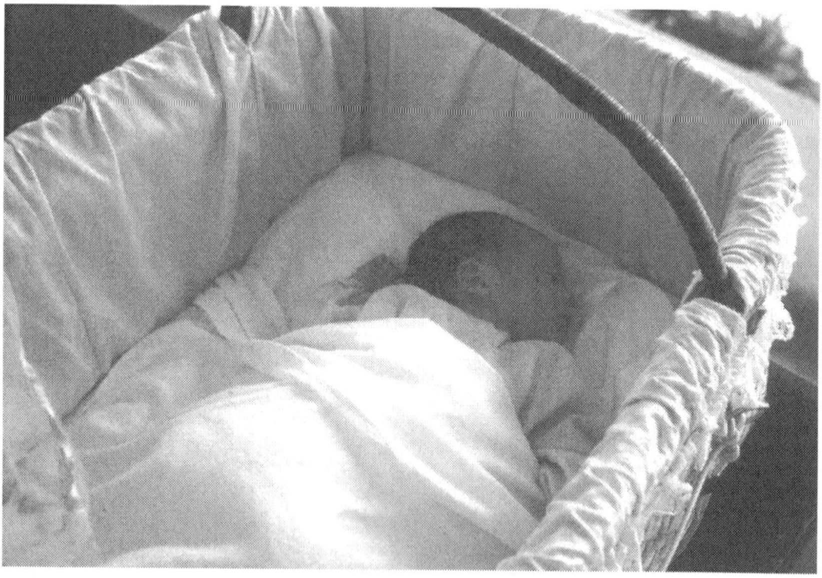

20.One-week-od Bruce.
Note the fine-mesh net on the left, the 'lace', and, under the lining, the padding off which the baby must often have bounced.

CHAPTER TEN

Mud/Sand tracks . Puncture repair. Baboon. Market.

The next morning our comic hotelier gave belly laughs as he pointed to long metal objects on Pythagoras's roof.
"What devilish implements are those?" he chortled. "Whatever they are, with them and full jerry cans up there, you'll be so top-heavy that a skid will turn you upside down and you'll be like a stranded dung beetle with its legs waving in the air."
We didn't appreciate his humour. The items that were causing him so much mirth were mud/sand tracks. We'd been to some trouble to acquire them since, like the Fish Basket, we'd had to devise them ourselves.

In Blantyre such possibly life-saving items were not obtainable, but since when had unavailability baulked us? Living in Malawi made us resourceful. People in Europe would never imagine how we managed without much that they considered absolutely indispensible. We accepted frequent water/electricity cuts, and knew that mechanical items, photographic equipment, domestic goods, cheese, chocolate, cream, sometimes butter, even flour, sugar etc. were often unavailable, so the lack of mere sand tracks hadn't fazed us!

Before we left Bob worked flat out earning money, while I prepared vehicle, food and assorted 'gear'. That included acquiring 'impossible' items. After a lot of rummaging through stockyards I finally discovered some very tough extruded iron mesh and had it cut into the semblance of 3 suitable strips. We couldn't afford the weight of a fourth. We just hoped that we would manage without it.

"You don't need those in Zaire," scorned Papadopolos. "If you have a strong arm and a sharp machete then bamboos, and there are usually plenty of those about, can be cut down.
But you have to watch out for the snakes that like to live in bamboo! The poles sink very cosily side by side into sludge and

provide satisfactory grip for tyres – so long as you place them at right angles to the line of desired motion."
"What if there are no bamboos around?" asked Bob.
"Then branches of trees have to do, but it is more difficult to collect suitable pieces and they don't give such successful purchase. They can also pop your tyres with incredibly sharp and strong, thorns or sticking-out twigs."
The thought of having to cut enough bamboos or tree branches was almost as bad as the idea of undoing the chains and lifting down the heavy tracks. We hoped like blazes that we'd have to do neither.

Well. O.K. – perhaps it wasn't crucial to carry *mud* tracks; but later, in the Sahara, with no vegetation, *sand* tracks would be a vital part of our equipment. These days travellers are so lucky. Lightweight roll-up mats are available.

The morning had dawned grey, misty and raw. Was it going to rain and ruin our chances of getting through LGT? After last night's late arrival and the proprietor's yarns we had gone late and yawning to bed leaving many routine chores undone. These now had to be completed, and Bruce, who was suffering from wind, added tension by crying.

It was not surprising that the Brat was afflicted with wind. He was fed as we bounced along and he soon learnt to stop the nipple from escaping by latching on tightly as he sucked. It gave him an extra point of support but he must have swallowed plenty of air each time he (frequently) lost his grip!

"The Greek's charging a shocking rate for changing Travellers' Cheques," said Bob. "I'm going to halve the sum we had intended to cash."
"I hope that we won't therefore end up penniless in some remote village."
"Ask him if there's somewhere to get petrol."
"In the days of prosperity," the hotelier said grandiloquently, "Beni had four petrol pumps. Three are burnt-out wrecks but the fourth works – when it has fuel. It's behind the hotel.
"And can we get a puncture repaired?"
"The petrol man will show you the way to the garage."

That sounded promising even though local mechanics invariably proved frighteningly incompetent and terribly slow. Strong arms were their chief qualification and having no equipment, they had to use ours, so Bob got out our big tyre levers, giant hammer and supplies of patches, glue, scrapers, matches...

The untended pump was on its last legs.

"I'll speak to that sad fellow sitting over there picking between his toes."

"Maybe he's got jiggers."

"I neither know nor care, and I don't propose to ask either!"

The toe scratcher was slow on the uptake but having at last understood our needs he summoned a man who brought a handle for the pump. It took ages, but to our relief Pythagoras's tank and all our jerry cans were filled. When we explained that we also needed to repair a puncture, the foot picker grudgingly climbed onto a mudguard and guided us to an old warehouse.

On an area of beaten mud a tame baboon, attached by a chain from her belt to a long run-wire seemed to be the only living creature in sight. We looked round mystified. Was this shed a garage? Where were the mechanics? Where was the person who would mend the puncture? There was no sign of the usual clutter of old car chasses to be cannibalised for spares? Our guide thumped on a corrugated iron door and a wrinkled Rumpelstiltskin-like face peered out through a crack.

An undefined metal section of some discarded vehicle hung by a length of wire from the branch of a tree. When we explained our mission Rumpelstiltskin emerged and belaboured the pendant with an iron pipe. The result was a loud though not untuneful racket.

"My man will come. You wait," said the ringer and vanished. Bob snorted, but we waited. Soon (by African standards) a man accompanied by two women turned up and banged on the barn door. The pregnant female had a few coins tied tightly in a small screw of material whose once-bright colours were smudged and muddy from being washed in a stream. The other woman had a baby on her back. All we could see of that was a small dark brown foot with a pink sole sticking out under each armpit, and the top of a head covered in frizzy black hair. Both girls were prone to the giggles!

Like a jack-in-the box the garage owner, emerged again, looked at the trio, and said:
"Here is the tyre mender."
The man agreed to work on our puncture and introduced each lady with the same words:
"This is my wife."
"This is my wife."
"They are going to market."
Seeing our surprise as we looked from one buxom lady to the other, the 'campanologist' shrugged his shoulders.
"What can we do? The wars killed thousands leaving five women to every man. Nobody practises monogamy."

Supposedly to ensure the supply of spare parts, imported cars were limited to twelve makes, but the few vehicles under repair, every tool and all spares, as well as even the useful sources of spare parts – dismembered car carcases – were secured *inside* the hangar with multiple padlocks. That spoke for itself. The scene inside was reminiscent of a Victorian workhouse. In semi-obscurity two men unceasingly pounded treadmills to turn wheels that provided power for the workshop lathe and grindstone. The baboon's life was probably more agreeable than those of the two sweating pedal-pounders.

"Will you supervise, or do you want to go to market with these good ladies to hunt for what may be available?" I asked tongue in cheek. I knew that my husband loathed shopping. "By the way, the hotel sold me some bread."
"Oh. Good. Seeing that you're better at selecting bananas," said Bob hypocritically, blenching at the thought of going to market, "I'll oversee the patching."

In these days of superb highways and modern tyres your car's probably never had a puncture. If you do pick up a nail it's just a question of handing the *tubeless* wheel over to the garage. With machines the repair is efficiently effected in a few minutes. It was very different in the depths of Africa in the seventies. Not only did tyres have inner tubes but every bit of the mend was labour intensive and each step had to be checked closely.

First, actually removing the rubber from the wheel hub was physical hard work – a wrestling ordeal. Then the repairman rummaged through a pile of discarded casings to select a suitable outer from which the gaiter was carved, filed smooth and glued into place. All holes in the inner tube had to be found. Big rents were obvious but to locate pinpricks the tube would be inflated (using *our* pump) and dipped into filthy water, then squeezed to observe where lines of bubbles emerged. When all punctures were adequately patched, the inner tube was replaced and the owner had to watch like a circling vulture to prevent the tube from being pinched. (Pinching a tube – catching the rubber between the tyre casing and the hub – cuts a slice through it.)

"But, if you disappear who'll look after Pythagoras while I'm overseeing the work?" asked my husband assuming that the tyre cobbling would be achieved inside the shed.

"*Pas d'problème,*" said Rumplestiltskin. "The man will manage the repair here, outside." He pointed under a nearby stunted tree to murky water in a half-barrel that was wedged with stones to prevent it from rolling.

Setting off with the two ladies I remembered lugging an increasingly heavy Bruce around Bujumbura and thought I'd take the chance to learn how to strap the baby onto my back. On our way north we'd been unable to wriggle out of accepting a present of a weird tablecloth. (Or was it a colossal tea towel?) The lurid-coloured flowers splodged all over it were so hideous that I had hidden this monstrosity in the clean nappy bag; but now it was just what was needed.

I asked the ladies to help me fix Bruce in situ. This provoked a deluge of giggles but one of them took Brat, held him up, and gazed admiringly. I swelled with pride until I realized that what she was enviously describing as 'very nice' was not my son but his nappy! The other woman pushed down my head till I was looking at my toes. Then Bruce was plonked

between my shoulder blades, his legs straightened, and in a moment they had expertly tied a few knots so I could stand upright again.
"It's not particularly comfortable," I objected.
"You'll get used to it," said Bob heartlessly. He didn't really approve of his son going piggyback like an African child. The baby didn't like it either and started to grizzle. Ignoring that, we set off in splendid style and I took good note of the way the wrap had been fixed. The knowledge might be useful later.

But Brat decided to give his fury full vent and I realised that I didn't fancy a stream of warm pee flowing down my spine! So he was unwrapped and we continued towards market with the now happy (triumphant) baby in my arms.

In a small, muddy area between huge trees local produce was spread over mats on the ground where sellers lay behind their wares and remained prone as they bargained with buyers. I've never seen such lackadaisical selling elsewhere. As usual everything was set out in small heaps or even individually, and I was glad I didn't need much for there was little on offer. I acquired 5 potatoes (1 heap) and a few small bananas. (Short ones are sweeter than longer varieties.)

Returning to the garage after a cheery tour I gently lobbed a banana at the baboon. With two hands she caught it adroitly against her chest; then her ears seemed to move backwards on her head indicating pleasure. Observing me keenly out of her intelligent, close-set eyes, the animal enjoyed her prize, skin and all.

The husband-of-two was having trouble replacing the outer casing onto its hub. We helped manipulate the tyre levers and tried to stop him from banging the wheel with terrible force. It was upsetting to see that he had made dents in several places. Inexpert hammering had produced dangerous kinks on the rim. But once the damage had been done there was nothing we could do to correct it. Later we suffered because of the bent hub.

We were feeling rather frazzled and definitely filled with foreboding as we crawled out of Beni heading towards LGT.

CHAPTER ELEVEN

L .G. T.

For hours the sludge, which was supposed to be a road, got worse and worse. But we kept fingers crossed because the region had been almost rainless for an unprecedented 3 days and so far today's misty threat hadn't turned into deluge. Sixty miles out from Beni, when we felt that the deterioration couldn't possibly increase, my heart did a double somersault. Ahead appeared a jam of monstrously over-loaded stationary lorries teetering on uneven ground. Bales and boxes, flapping tarpaulins, sheets of ripped plastic, bicycles, barrels and furniture clung to the mountainous luggage. Much overhung the sides. The juggernauts were lingering while their drivers gathered courage before advancing into LGT. Would we have to join the line and, like them, wait in fear?

"There's a bamboo pole closing the road – beyond the queue of trucks."

We bounced on towards the barrier till, a long way ahead of the wagons, we could make out the start of a deep and dreadful cut with irregular mud walls from which boulders protruded.

We were stopped, of course.

"You cannot pass."

"It is forbidden."

"Nothing can get through except – *maybe* – big vehicles with many pushers."

"You must turn back."

"We will not allow you to go on."

"You will become broken in the middle. Then our convoys will not achieve passage."

Drivers of the stranded behemoths snarled and ordered us in no uncertain terms to go back. Their tones held scarcely veiled threats that they would physically prevent us from trying to thread the canyon. They frightened us but we responded as staunchly as possible:

"We only want to approach and look at the famous site." (Liars!)

Discussion! But we had little choice. Pride and obstinacy barred us from turning round!

A small gang of labourers was lethargically trying to pour rocks and muck into the biggest of the potholes. They'd been doing this for years with no visible improvement to the terrain. Wearing a fantastic, wide-brimmed hat cut from a cardboard box, their '*capitaine,*' with drug-reddened eyes, had his price. Finally worn down and taken aside into bushes, he raised his ingenious headgear to scratch, and then accepted 20 Rhodesian King Size cigarettes. Smiling grimly, certain we would make a U turn, he lifted the pole and authorised us to "Go. Look."

36. Red eyes and a very fetching cardboard hat.

Like navigating a solidified stormy sea we ventured slowly and painfully across what seemed to be a building site just abandoned by bulldozers, till ahead opened the horrendous 'defile'. It was so long that it even incorporated a lengthy curve. A truck waiting at the far end was invisible. The prospect was terrifying.

"Take the cine," said Bob in a strangled voice as clutching Bruce to my chest, I left Pythagoras. Stepping down onto orange-coloured mud I was swamped by labourers crowding round to examine the baby. When the chattering workers were advised to move away because we planned to advance, they parted with alacrity fearing for their lives and, unlike the vicious drivers further back, they helped me to climb onto the small cliff that edged the side of LGT. From there, by simply taking one sideways step, I could have stood on the upright jerry cans and other paraphernalia that rattled about on Pythag's roof as he fought his way along the passage.

Our luck was unbelievable. Not only was LGT almost dry but cowardly juggernauts had not yet started to plough along its length. We were perfectly familiar with the routine of slamming down the red knob when we needed 4-wheel drive but we had seldom (so far! – Zaire altered that) had to resort simultaneously to the yellow knob that gave us reduced (stronger) gears.

I watch with sucked-in breath as, looking fiercely determined, Bob selects both knobs. He switches on the engine. The motor issues deep growls as reduced gear cuts in. Bob allows Pythagoras to creep forward.

They start down the chasm. The car is lurching dreadfully – swaying. The ruts are deep. Actually they're not ruts. Ruts cut into a road in more or less parallel lines. The bottom of this ravine is wounded in all directions and pitted randomly with epic holes. Little mountains rise up like an evil illness.

CRASH! Pythag hits the left wall and bounces away. For some seconds it looks as if the vehicle's about to topple but the other wall catches the roof rack a terrible blow and rights the car. Bob's skinny arms swirl and twist. He can't hope to avoid the broken exhaust pipes, sump cages, springs and other unidentifiable extrusions that project from the cement-like hillocks of caked mud and from the sides. It's not feasible to expect any driver to avoid those. That has to be left to fate. I can only pray that they don't cause irreparable damage.

Appalled, filming automatically, I stumble through the thick vegetation that lines the sides of Le Grand Trou. I am desperate not to trip and fall into the abyss, but determined to record everything on celluloid. The cine whirrs and I gaze, horrified and mesmerised through the viewfinder. My finger presses instinctively on the GO button. This is using up a helluva lot of film! Photography is so expensive that usually we are extremely economical. But this is beyond belief momentous. If Pythagoras makes it out of LGT it will be an Historic Event!

Another WALLOP! Our vehicle leaps off a rock and staggers onto a wall. CRUNCH! The giant transports have worn depressions that are wider apart than Pythag's axle span. To avoid letting his tyres slither into the eroded tracks Bob must keep one or other wheel up on the central spine. With one side so much higher than the other the Land Rover leans awfully. His wheels must not slip sideways or he'll be abruptly immobilised with his belly impaled on the bristly spikes that run centrally all along the solidified "river", wheels spinning uselessly in space – always supposing that the engine hasn't died.

Seeming to bound from one protuberance to the next hazard the car also sashays violently from side to side. At least the canyon walls prevent him from capsizing. He jolts forward, juddering, constantly striking first one rocky bank and then rebounding off the other. The engine's grinding noises echo between those small bulwarks. As the underside hits obstacles there are dreadful whacks and thumps.

Terrorised, dreading what might happen, I pray that Pythagoras won't stall or an axle break. Scarcely daring to hope that the undercarriage will escape damage I will *the vehicle to stay in one piece and keep moving.*

Watchers are static as if paralysed, uncharacteristically silent. Men stand poised, still holding aloft just-emptied baskets from which they'd just tipped soil. Breathing stops. Hot, humid air shimmers. Monster trees loom like statues. Bob's movement is at a snail's pace – but at least it's maintained. Luckily liquid mud occurs only in pockets between the solidified chunks so isn't extensive enough for the car to need momentum or to cause skids that are even more desperate than the sideways slides. The driver's body corkscrews as the steering wheel wrenches him left and right. He fights every inch of the way: a horrendous sight. The Greek's acting was nothing compared to this.

BUT! He got through – and to be certain, Bob took staggering Pythagoras, some distance further along the ghastly track. I was mindless with relief – and disbelief. It seemed an age since the Land Rover had nosed its noisy way slowly into the ravine. I looked down and was amazed to realise that I was gripping Bruce. For all the care I had given the baby during that aeon, he might as well have been a rag doll. Luckily his head was uppermost and he wasn't blue, so presumably he was still alive. I hadn't squeezed all the air out of him.

Suddenly cheers exploded from the accumulated audience. There were yells from the repair gang. Ululating women, waving headscarves, appeared from dense jungle where they had been hiding. Everyone was clapping. Compared with the waiting giants Pythagoras was a mere flea; and the insect had achieved the impossible! Unlike the monster lorries that just *ground* their ways *through* obstacles, our car had *jumped* from obstruction to problem and juddered *over* them all.

I could scarcely believe that, as I filmed, oblivious to everything but Pythagoras's painful and shuddering advance, I had neither fallen into the undergrowth through which I was struggling, nor slipped over the edge into the small 'ravine'. Gesticulating and scattering sweets to show gratitude, I ran after the vehicle.

While Bob looked anxiously out of the window, waiting tensely, I studied it from all angles searching for any visible damage. My voice had seized up but I managed to croak:

"Seems O.K."

Later my husband told me:

"You sounded so casual! As if you'd just examined something entirely unimportant!"

Breathing an ENORMOUS sigh of thanks to the spirits of the place, I hopped in, still clutching baby and camera, amazed again to find that I still had Bruce intact!

Waving, and vastly relieved, we chugged off and, as soon as we were well away from the scene, we stopped to mop our brows, replace the Fish Basket dweller, and to celebrate with thermos tea.

Although we were shaken and still shaking WE WERE PAST *LE GRAND TROU*!!!

Ours was the first vehicle through for a very long time and we heard later that for some months more, until much repair work had been achieved, the giant pothole remained totally impassable for normal sedan cars – not that we ever saw any of those other than tottering or dead relics in towns.

Feeling reprieved and rather faint we swapped places and continued our trek.

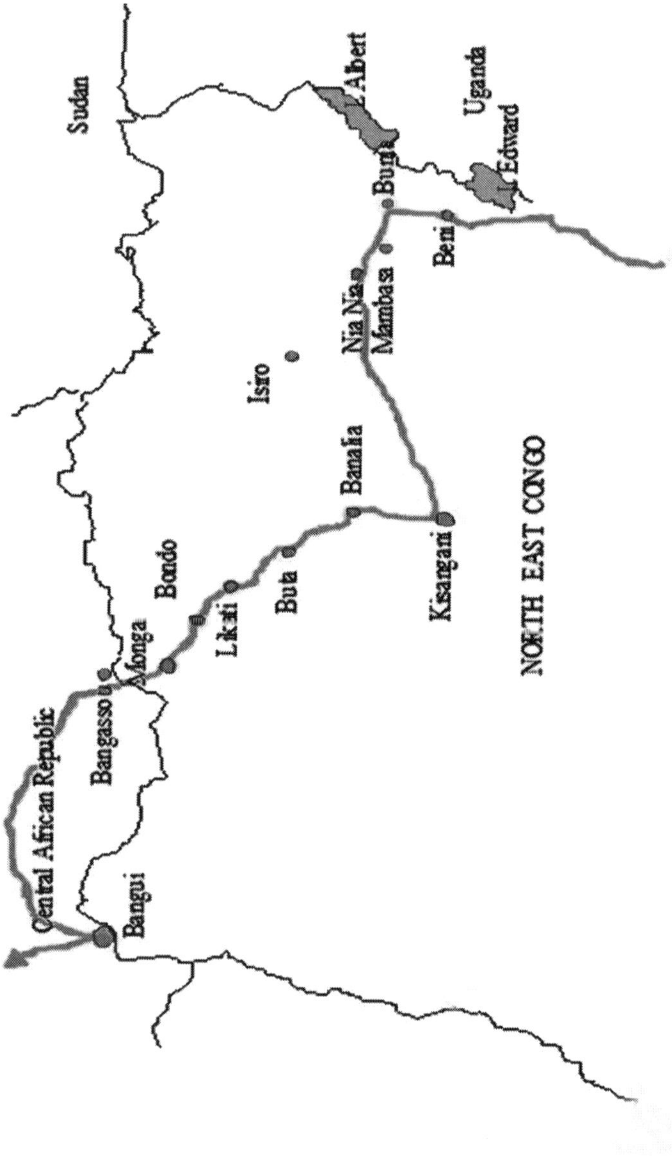

21. Showing our route from south of Beni to Bangui

CHAPTER TWELVE

Railway? Land Rovers' Convoy. Beetle.

The shocking 'roads' that we had so far struggled along from Bukavu to Beni existed – or just survived – only because of contact with Uganda. Now, the track deteriorated to ghastly and we had to plunge through real jungle on the only route that was open. Of course it depends what you mean by 'open'. Many travellers considered the way completely IMpassable.

It wasn't only highways that had vanished. There was the story of a biologist seeking specimens deep in the forest during the late nineteen-sixties. Feeling something unnaturally rectangular beneath his foot he told his workers:

"Dig away the undergrowth. Find out what this is."

"A railway sleeper! How on earth did *that* reach the middle of the jungle?"

"It is attached to something," said his men.

"Oh? Investigate."

"Two long pieces of metal, Sir. Going out on both sides, Sir. The gods must have placed this big juju. How else could such enormous lengths of iron exist?"

Miles of railway line were buried deep beneath roots and burgeoning vegetation. The contrast between Congo's former amenities and its 1971 dereliction was almost too great to be described.

Beyond LGT we saw people only at very small, widely separated settlements hacked from Rain Forest. These were surly folk with drug- or booze- induced blurry eyes who rarely smiled. Women always greatly outnumbered men. Sometimes solitary males just sat leaning against tree trunks, looking stupefied – which they probably were – on homemade 'medicine' or beer that everywhere seemed to be available in great quantities. Drunken policemen and armed soldiers were terrifying, only too obviously best shunned. Each threw his weight about in efforts to impress the whores all over the country, but especially at 'hostelries' run by those 'ladies'.

The mud was thick, the ruts deep, and branches on each side of the track were sweeping Pythagoras with enormous leaves. To our amazement we saw the vegetation ahead being pushed aside by an oncoming bumper. Another vehicle! Good heavens! And it was *moving*! Probably our jaws dropped. A truck capable of advancing was rare *in settlements*. Elsewhere we sometimes didn't see another viable vehicle of any sort for days on end. Now a convoy of three Land Rovers came battling towards us. In various stages of disbelief and shock everybody stopped and clambered out onto rich red sludge. Nine pairs of disparaging eyes stared at us in astonishment as there was a moment of silence while we gaped blankly at each other.

"I say! Aren't they scruffy!" I whispered unkindly.

"You shouldn't say so," muttered Bob sarcastically with a scornful grin. "They're really 'pukka sahibs' and identically kitted out. Look at their special London-made safari outfits. I'm surprised they aren't wearing Dr Livingstone caps with flaps down the backs of their necks. "

"I don't care. They're horrendously grimy, and 'frightfully British'. I bet that khaki material is sweaty hot! – And it must take HOURS to dry – Incredible to meet such types here."

The travellers gazed at our 'ordinary' (but reasonably clean) cotton garb patronisingly. I washed our clothes regularly and Bob shaved every morning. We found that looking as presentable as possible helped our own morale and also eased our passage in all sorts of situations. Bob and I goggled when they produced a primus and with unpractised difficulty, at last persuaded it to work. We opened a thermos flask that we'd filled that morning using water boiled on our campfire. Then, very British-ly (!), we all imbibed tea together – without cucumber sandwiches!

As I prepared some plebeian slices I had enormous trouble keeping an outsize beetle with massive claw-like antennae out of the cheese box. He was a glorious creature, colourful, huge, and doggedly determined to investigate our food. I picked him up and threw him into bushes. A shuddering woman pointed:

"The insects are absolutely appalling! How can you touch it like that? It completely filled your hand! Ugh! Look! It's dropped a spot of liquid."
I wiped the yellow-brown droplet off my palm and discovered it had caused a tiny blister that soon vanished.

Are beetles arthropods? (See the Appendix – page181 – for a definition). Yes; and therefore potential carriers of Ebola. Since we didn't fall ill we must have been lucky in our dealings with the many splendid specimens that we met along our way.

Compared to the pukka sahibs' three long-wheel-based Land Rovers, our solitary, stubby Pythagoras seemed dwarfed and vulnerable. Tales of their troubles made us quake with fears of what we had to face, though later we wondered what they'd been talking about.
"The mire's impossibly thick," they complained. "We keep on getting stuck."
"You'll never get through without others to pull you out of bogs, and to care for you when you fall ill. Good grief! You haven't even got a winch!"
"How can you possibly imagine that just two of you – and in only one vehicle – are going to manage?"

Their carrot-haired, wildly bearded leader, whom they seemed to worship, thought they were very soon going to emerge onto good roads and they tried to impress us with their past achievements. We could have disillusioned them and scored heavily at that game by mentioning LGT, which they were about to face; but stunned by their unusual attitude we felt it wasn't worth bothering and kept silent. They seemed ignorant of the imminent obstacle, probably because they didn't speak French.

Their reports were scarcely encouraging:
"I can't stand this overpowering vegetation."
"The locals are most unpleasant – and so primitive! We've run out of insecticide and we had our spare wheel pinched. We haven't been able to buy a thing!"
What did they expect? A.A boxes? The Admirable Creighton? Supermarkets and garages behind every clump of bulrushes?
"Tom saw a terrible snake!"

Immediately our attention picked up. "What sort?"
"Good heavens! I don't care. The only good snake's a dead one!"
We were scandalized but still curious.
"What colour? How long? Where was it – in a tree? Elephant grass? Bamboos?"
"Oh just *there*, you know, close to the track. Oof! *Horrible*!"
We were obviously not going to get any serious details.

Unlike other people, this lot were completely uninterested in the baby. Just one woman glanced briefly and remarked:
"It won't survive," before turning back to her tea.

The bonny little bundle was probably the healthiest of our group. He always had as much as he wanted to suck – on demand, – was bathed every evening of the whole 3.5-month-long trip, except for about seven nights in total when we were short of water or just too exhausted; and he could never feel abandoned or lonely for he was constantly with one or both parents. We'd had no chance to weigh him but it was obvious that he was growing at a pleasing rate, and he spent his time asleep or gurgling happily, grizzling only when he felt that insufficient attention was being paid to him. Bob was seriously concerned that we were spoiling his son but couldn't think of how to introduce character-building restraints into the Brat's life.

We were glad to move on from the ultra-British party with their introverted and insular outlooks, but as leaves closed in on the track behind us and the other group vanished, suddenly I felt very much alone and defenceless. Instead of gazing in wonder at the enormous trees and heart-stopping mud I noticed our surroundings with fear. However were we to get through these walls of unrelenting greenery?

There was no conversation in Pythagoras for a very long time. Was Bob struggling with similar feelings?

CHAPTER THIRTEEN

Murderous culverts. Royal Engineers. Ebola!

LGT may have been a spectacular hazard. The astounding *aperitif* was an attack of smaller but much more blood-curdling *petits trous* (small holes). They looked so insignificant and innocuous! In fact they didn't "look" at all because they were virtually invisible. Until you were on top of one you never saw that a rivulet sliced through the road and that there was a murderous, narrow, un-bridged crevasse with vertical sides just about to disappear below your tyres.

It was quite usual to find gaps right across sections of *bad* track – we accepted those as fair game because on rotten roads one had to be ready for anything. We learnt to make light of bridgeless streams; but it seemed very unkind of fate to have sprinkled the murderous splits on a rare stretch of highway apparently made of 'good' dirt. Those deep cracks could easily have been our downfall.

We hit the initial evil culvert-that-wasn't when we were going at what, in those days, we considered 'speed' (10 mph!). We just never saw the cut; but we fell into it with a double tremendous CRASSSSSH! BANG! – First the front wheels and then the rear tyres dropped and rebounded. The engine stalled. Luckily momentum carried us over the gap, so Pythag didn't remain with wheels stuck in space. The double big bumps first DOWN and then UP were ENORMOUS. They were followed by a final downwards smash and consequent smaller bounces.

The result was truly remarkable! The nappy bucket – naturally – shared its contents generously. The machete abandoned its close association with the back of the driver's seat, shot out of its slot forward of the food crate, and soared as if being brandished by a mad invisible dervish. Thank goodness it didn't plunge down onto Bruce! Luckily it landed harmlessly, slicing open the bag of root vegetables. Those, of course, scattered and bounded about. Three small suitcases, which usually lay in a neat wedged-in pile below the Fish Basket, *all turned right over*. That seemed past belief and we trembled when we realised that the Brat's cradle might also have capsized like the suitcases beneath it. One burst open and spewed its contents everywhere. Radio, tape recorder, films – used and new – sweets and cigarettes, binoculars, hussif, notebooks and other such items rocketed up to the roof and then fell all over the place like enormous confetti. Solid rain made a great clatter. The 25-litre plastic jerry can full of water – although very heavy and tightly fixed – didn't manage to escape from its corner but unbelievably within that confined crevice, it was inverted. We *never* understood how things could turn right over yet remain in situ. Packets and tins of food deserted their crate and took wings.

Bruce's basket proved its worth. Its two handles must have helped to deviate falling objects. The *elastic straps* and fine *net* that were stretched across its top caught a variety of items thus preventing the baby from suffering a blitzkrieg. Presumably they also stopped him from taking flight like other luggage in the back of Pythagoras. Bruce himself was scarcely disturbed by the violent upheaval. He woke and started waving his limbs but never uttered any sound. Was he just too surprised – stunned perhaps – to give voice? Maybe he considered we had really done him proud for his motto was now: "The bouncier the better!" The smoother the driving the less happy he became, and yelled loud displeasure. When we started leap-frogging about again he would shut up! Had we addled his brains with all the shaking and bumping?

In the front of the stationary, but still juddering vehicle Bob and I were shocked breathless and speechless. After a second or two my husband rubbed his yet-again bruised head and remarked in a cracked voice:

"Ladies and gentlemen, the 'plane has landed. Please take great care when opening the overhead lockers."

Of course we had no overhead lockers. We never allowed luggage to go above the back of the seats. This gave us an unimpeded view behind Pythagoras, few visible goods to entice thieves, and it also meant that nothing was higher than the baby's cradle so there wasn't anything to tumble down onto him. (Flying up and subsequently falling was a different kettle of fish, which we had not anticipated and which repeated bounces taught us that no amount of careful packing could prevent). We emerged shakily to examine our vehicle from all angles, including from below, and were astounded to see no obvious damage. Good old Pythag!

"What luck that we've got no eggs!" I said with feeling. Having to scrape a huge scrambled mess from all our goods would have been purgatory!

There were about two dozen of these horrors and, although after the first invisible crack, our 'speed' dropped to a crawl and we drove with utmost care, we still got caught by another – fortunately with less drastic consequences. After these *petits trous* and their huge brother, LGT, we rounded a bend and quite literally gasped. There, in the middle of thick jungle, far from any civilisation, cutting a swathe through enormous trees and tangled undergrowth was a length of absolutely superb tarmac.

"Careful!" cautioned Bob.

We had learnt by bitter experience that 'Good' roads usually hid treacherous terrors. Wondering, and very cautiously, we advanced along this amazing asphalt. Then – were our eyes really seeing lots of men working on the highway? – In this land where nothing was ever repaired or maintained? – What was more, they were *white* navvies – in a country where only locals – and only women at that – carried out manual labour! Not really believing what we could see, we stopped to pass the time of day and to find out what in Hades they were doing? Then came the third shock. We had by now become used to the Africanised Belgian-type French spoken round these parts so it nearly knocked us backwards to hear strong cockney emerging from those weather-blistered red throats. It transpired that toiling in the steaming jungle was a party of British Royal Engineers

"We've been b---y well lent to Zaire to achieve the construction of this f----g road," they complained. Poor fellows! They didn't like the rain! They didn't like the heat! They hated the insects and, with justification, they were absolutely terrified of mosquitoes and tsetse flies. Their particular nightmare was Warrior Ants. I wonder what length of highway they completed and how much remained of their efforts when wars afterwards repeatedly smashed through that region. We heard later that they managed to deprive Zaire of LGT, the biggest pothole in the world. I don't think it – or their efforts – ever got into the Guinness Book of Records.

The deadly *petits trous,* their monstrous 'brother', LGT, and the amazing bit of perfect highway all came within a twenty-mile stretch. We couldn't complain of monotony!

That day we passed out from beautiful Kivu Province where we had met on the whole friendly, sometimes Swahili-speaking, Africans into the Pygmy-inhabited jungle that seemed totally deserted of any kind of human.

Like the Royal Engineers I was terrified of Warrior Ants. I prayed that our zips would keep them out of the tent. We did see multiple ranks of these creatures but they didn't attack us. There were also lots of smaller ant varieties all scurrying about apparently desperate to conduct business under decaying debris or up tree trunks. Many of them, like unflagging standard bearers, carried aloft leaves, their eggs, pupae or chrysalises. Dropping from overhead, earwigs, some absolutely gargantuan, were even more repulsive. Other creepy crawlies were too numerous to mention.

One evening I gave a small, shocked squawk as something hard and segmented scuttled from under my foot to slide away under leaf mould. Instinctively jumping sideways, I gave an equally involuntary croak of "Scorpion!"

Bob reacted predictably. *Almost* looking up he said:

"Careful!" and turned back to his diary writing.

When the creature then broke cover, scurried up a tree trunk and stopped, I realised that a crab and I were observing each other with equal interest.

"No," I corrected myself. "It's a crab!"

"Don't be silly. We're *miles* from the sea. "

Bob paused, thought, and added:
"Well over a thousand – at the very least."
"It's a land crab then – or a freshwater thing."

51. The enlarged claw is used for fighting and for pulling food into its mouth. It's hard to understand that arthropods – such as crabs, spiders, etc – are potential Ebola carriers

A boy of about ten, though it was difficult to judge ages in this land of malnutrition, laughed. Then crouching and hunting, he surprisingly quickly, came up with another crab. To my horror he crushed it with a stone and threw it into a less overgrown patch.
"Watch," he told me. But I didn't have time to stand and observe a dead crustacean so I moved to continue supper preparations. The lad, however, had more patience and in a few minutes, chuckling, he followed me and pointed.
"Come. Look!"

It was disgusting! Several more crabs had congregated and were tearing their dead fellow apart. Greedily the cannibals clawed pieces of its body into their mouths.
"Yuk!" I said and turned away.
I didn't know then that arthropods, e.g. crabs, (see Appendix) carry Ebola.

Our guardian angels, working hard as usual, persuaded us to avoid another night drive. So instead of driving on to Station de L'Epulu which we had hoped to reach by evening, we stopped at a settlement called Mambasa. Gosh! We were lucky!

As explained in Chapter 1 we thus escaped the virus of frightful Ebola Disease that was then seething in the Epulu region. This fearsome illness, which is easily spread by contact of body liquids, causes fever, vomiting, and so much internal bleeding that the death rate caused by rapid dehydration was until recently 90%. To date (2015) there is no known cure. Not formally investigated until 1976, Ebola has erupted for many years and it continues to recur from time to time. As explained in the Introduction (page iv), in 1971 there was virtually no transport. People did not move about so Ebola outbreaks killed the locals and then, for lack of human carriers, usually died away itself. Nowadays, of course, we all know how that has changed!

Don't just skim through those words and skip onto the next paragraph. No. Stop. Think about the ghastly sufferings of Ebola's victims already dead, and still being killed today. We were incredibly lucky not to have had that virus sneezed, coughed, bitten or otherwise injected into our blood streams. By buying this book you have helped M.S.F. to fight Ebola.

In 1976, and again in 2012 the horrible illness exploded in Isiro district (to which we were now heading), but it was undoubtedly bubbling in the region for very many years before that. In 2014 its killing tentacles erupted into West Africa.

On Tuesday 2nd November 1971 we had started from Beni. When we switched off the engine at Mambasa we were only 84 miles from Beni, by the old (direct) road, – now defunct. However, due to the tortuous nature of the detour, Pythagoras had covered 142 difficult miles during the long, and eventful day. BUT we were beyond LGT and that filled our hearts with relieved joy.

We relaxed, thinking: "Sufficient unto the day" would be the evils of the future, and didn't suspect how terrifyingly evil the very next day would become.

33. Before crossing LGT and then plunging into the *real* jungle we came across some amazing but short-lived stretches of splendid road like this. Alas, they were blighted by hidden and treacherous hazards! Note the long vertical (black) bundle to the left of the back door of Pythagoras. It held the Hi-lift jack and it features in a catastrophe later in the story.

4. The picture on the next page shows a much more typical road surface. That photo was taken outside Goma to record a highly **A-typical** event: road works in progress!

CHAPTER FOURTEEN

Mambasa and Father Laurent.

Mambasa had a tiny mission engulfed by towering jungle. From Bob's diary that evening:

"Tonight at Mambasa we are really in the Equatorial Forest where it rains for most of the year. It is quite incredibly humid. Everything is moist and chill. Occasionally, when heavy clouds part a lovely full moon shines down on us from above a 'feather duster' of palms. The jungle all round is very thick but this clearing was presumably opened up in the old days for the original mission buildings, which were destroyed during the massacres. They are being rebuilt.

Pythagoras has now covered 2,127 miles: about half of the distance from Blantyre to Zaria, (Nigeria) - where we hope to visit Daphne's brother and his family. After that looms the awesome prospect of the Sahara. I think we are both rather scared about that.

We have passed through and out of Malawi, Zambia, Tanzania, Burundi - all currently dry areas where the Rains are still pending, into the region where - theoretically - the Rains are nearly ending. For the next week or so we shall be desperately hoping to avoid late season downpours."

Pot-bellied Father Laurent, with a tremendous hawk nose jutting from his thin face, allowed us to camp in the large glade of the Mambasa Mission. Much clutter of construction-in-

progress lay scattered among boulders, bushes and bamboo huts.
"Be careful," the priest told us. "There are leopards about."
"Where have you arrived from?" he asked, puzzled.
"Beni."
Father Laurent gasped.
"You passed *Le Grand Trou?*"
"Yes."
"Truly the Good Lord must have been with you."
"It was quite exciting!"
"Je m'en doute pas!" (I have no doubt of that!) "And with the bébé! I felicitate you!"
Still muttering about our luck and Providence he retired to his modest mud house.

As we finished erecting the tent, Bob said:
"We needn't bother with the flysheet tonight. It's going to be dry."
Surprised, I looked at the mists swirling round tree trunks and at the damp miasma hovering everywhere.
"Going to be dry?" I echoed like a Zombie.
"Well, look overhead."
Above the thick canopy I could see no clear sky, and no starlight; but neither were there the tremendous banks of cumulus, which on previous nights in the Congo had usually dumped torrential and thunderous downpours upon us. Perhaps they were going to take a night off. So we skipped the tedious chore of spreading the flysheet over the tent.

Yet, at 2.30 am, when I fed a hungry Bruce, I was worried to find drops of water falling on my face.
"Bob!"
"Wasamarra?"
"Rain!"
As I hauled the flysheet out of Pythagoras my husband's language at these 'glad' tidings can probably be imagined. The tent was extremely rainproof even without the flysheet, so since I'd felt drops, presumably one of the nightly deluges had already hit us particularly hard and would doubtless recur. With

no desire to become even wetter than we already were, we unhappily hoisted the external cover.
"We're supposed to be *missing* the worst of the Rains!" I grumbled.
"We are," came the disgruntled reply. "At any other time of the year it'd be a hundred times worse."
Sleepily and confused he looked round.
"Doesn't seem to be any sign of flood – past, present or to come."

The next morning, when locals confirmed that in jungle terms it had indeed been a 'dry' night, we concluded:
"The drops of liquid must have been caused by a slight fall in temperature: enough to produce condensation of the soaked air outside and inside the tent."

We breakfasted as villagers straddling poles or sitting on partially carved stones, participated in their daily, dawn, open-air service. The sound of their deep African voices rumbling through impressive trees was moving. With that over, Father Laurent looked round and yelled:
"Undro! Where's my belt?"

Evidently Undro couldn't locate the good Father's accessory but, being an enterprising lad, he chopped a length of creeper from a tree and proffered that. The priest grunted his thanks – or was it irritation? With accustomed ease he used the length of creeper to hitch his once-white robe above his knees. Then he set-to with his flock chipping rocks for a new church. Every now and again he impatiently yanked his garment even higher to the status of a revealing mini skirt, and the green smear round his waist became more pronounced.
"I'm sure he'd rather work almost naked – like his parishioners," I remarked.
"Certainly if I was compelled to wear a cassock in this climate I wouldn't have a stitch of anything underneath," agreed Bob.
In the past I had wondered whether certain parts of celibate men atrophied through lack of use. Now was my chance to investigate. Instead, instinctively, I stupidly averted my eyes.

My husband was still gazing at the priest.
"That chap must be a rare specimen," he said sombrely. "In the sixties most of the white people, especially monks and nuns, were slaughtered."
"He must be incredibly brave and persevering." I agreed, adding: "...and have oodles of faith."
But I didn't voice the thought that also occurred to me:
'We have 'white' skins and 1971 isn't all that far removed from the sixties!'
In fact Father Laurent was the only *white* priest that we came across in the jungly regions. Other missionaries and churchmen who we met in outlying stations were from local tribes.

"Just look at the sandals he's stomping about in!"
"Amazing! Just badly cut chunks of old car tyres roughly cobbled together!"
Later this form of cheap and easily obtainable footwear became known as 'million milers'. Its popularity spread in Africa and then deliberately clumsy, factory-moulded copies became the rage among Hippie types in the West. Father Laurent's were the first we'd ever seen and hideously authentic!

This character, with leaves and flowers dangling like strange rosaries from his creeper belt, swore at his flock with amazing fluency in several languages. The workers' deeply black faces split into huge grins, and showed great expanses of gleaming white teeth as they laughed, chattered, riposted and obeyed.
"This church will soon be rebuilt," we agreed.

Even the baby, supported on my knee as I sat on a tree stump squeezing lemon juice over my piece of breakfast pawpaw, seemed to notice Father Laurent.
"Look," I said. "Bruce's head sometimes moves as if he's watching the body that's emitting such loud noises."
"Probably in amazement – if a baby is capable of such a reaction," replied Bob busy spreading marmalade on a piece of Beni bread.

We were pleased that the Brat had definitely proved that he could hold up his head, move it intentionally and notice what was going on round about. It was good to know that he was making positive progress despite his unconventional conditions.

When Bob moved away I noticed out of the corner of my eye a tot, in nothing but an abbreviated and ragged shirt, approaching warily, so I smiled, and holding out a hand said: "Hello," whereupon he jumped like a frightened duiker and scurried several steps backwards. I pretended not to notice as he then crept up again. Something was fascinating him.

Other children were eyeing me and very slowly drawing closer. It was like a game of Grandmother's Footsteps. If I looked at them they squealed in genuine fright and withdrew. When I gazed the other way, they shuffled forwards. The original youngster in the lead stood for a long time with one finger in his mouth, till suddenly filled with bravado, he dashed towards Bruce and stroked the baby's bare leg. The infant toddled back and studied his hand. Other kids followed his example, first in terrified silence and then giggling. Later Father Laurent told me that they were trying to find out why the baby wasn't black.

This was the only place we saw children lively enough to play and be curious. Truly this pastor was having a marvellous effect upon his flock. As the youngsters became braver the game developed and soon they, their parents and I were laughing our heads off.

"Undro tells me there's a petrol pump in the hamlet."
"I can't believe it. Such a tuppenny ha'penny, run-down settlement..." Bob scoffed, looking round sceptically.
"Well, Undro says his brother works for the pump owner."
('Brother' could refer to any male relative or special friend.)
"Let's top up anyway if it's possible."

That was an excellent move. We saw no other pump, functioning or otherwise, until, 14 eventful hours later, with only three ten-minute pauses en route, we reached Kisangani 342 miles further on. Despite our by now blasé attitude to primitive sources of petrol, we stood gob-stoppered by the astounding palaver that Undro's 'brother' had to achieve before the nozzle could be persuaded to disgorge. It took him 20 minutes to prime the pump and the stuff that finally emerged was like pea soup! Thank heavens we had a filter in our huge petrol funnel!

"Good success!" said the man as he poured his ghastly ooze through our strainer into Pythagoras's tank.

"What do you mean?"

"You passed Le Gran Trou. Felicitations! Everyone is amazed."

"How do you know?"

"Last night two lorries arrived in Mambasa. They came from Uganda and had been waiting at the big hole for many-many days. Their drivers told us how you jumped across the dangers. They followed behind you."

"Oh. Did any other trucks get through?"

"I think one more went the other way – towards Beni."

He added nonchalantly:

"Three Land Rovers await on this side of the hole."

We knew who that lot was!

"Why are they waiting?" we asked as innocently as possible.

"They fear."

"Oh." How news does leap about the jungle!

So we had broken the jam, and for brave travellers the total isolation of Kivu Province from the rest of Zaire was over – till the next rainstorms!

CHAPTER FIFTEEN

The petrol funnel

There's a funny story connected with that enormous petrol funnel. It happened way back at the border from Zambia into Tanzania. A huge flattened area of dust was filled with behemoths carrying diesel oil and equipment for building the 'Chink Link': a railway that was to join Zambia and Tanzania. The wonderful Chinese project has since unfortunately degenerated into a white elephant. (Perhaps you saw the sad BBC4 documentary.) Carrying our papers Bob disappeared into clouds of billowing sand to complete border formalities while I stayed to guard the car and the baby from scores of circulating idlers with sharp eyes and shifty hands.

My husband returned eventually, hot and furious, grumbling about the surly treatment he'd received.

"...and they won't stamp your travel documents without actually *seeing* you," he finished with a snort.

So, armed with papers and permits, I reluctantly took my turn in a slow-moving queue of mal-odorous, betel-nut-chewing, sweating, swearing, spitting, shoving lorry drivers. In due course I was livid too.

"Because Bruce is on my passport Immigration Officials won't let us proceed till they're sure he's really with us!" I muttered through clenched teeth when I got back to Pythagoras. Easing the sleeping baby from the Fish Basket, I carried him past jeering yobs, through all-penetrating dust and filthy fumes from truck exhausts. He woke, sneezed and yowled.

While the distressed baby and I fought through queues, Bob was the recipient of lewd remarks and lascivious laughter. Tied on top of the spare wheel on Pythagoras's bonnet, and sticking up vertically, our huge inverted fuel funnel attracted much attention. The funnel was essential throughout the African part of our journey. Not only did it incorporate a filter to catch floating bodies that arrive with the petrol from jerry cans and also from many country pumps, but liquids don't flow horizontally; so when refuelling on long stretches between available supplies it was virtually impossible, without its directional ability, to pour from a spoutless jerry can into the fuel tank through the almost vertical hole in the side of the car.

The general levity and sex-charged remarks were mystifying until we discovered that the metal 'cone' had been taken to be a rhino horn – a supposed notable aphrodisiac. Indeed it did look very much as if Pythag had sprouted a pointed tuft of matted hair on his "nose". The fact that we had a baby with us only increased the bawdy racket.

Consternation! Rhinos are fiercely protected!

Customs officers came to the car like an archaeological dig team. With malicious grins they upturned everything and checked each number they could think of on vehicle and cameras. They regaled us with fearsome reports of our proposed route through Burundi, and horror stories about some mysterious 'Huge hole' in Zaire's roads.

"You will not manage to pass!" they told us joyfully.

One of our big cartons was full of tins and packets. I had spent hours carefully arranging them so they would be available over the coming weeks in the order in which we planned to eat their contents. My heart shrivelled as officials scattered the boxes of meat, fish, vegetables, Ryvita and soup.

As a final sting they announced:

"In Tanzania *all* Land Rovers count as commercial vehicles which must display special licences on windscreens. You must buy a licence in Mbeya."

"But Mbeya is 70 miles out of our way. Can't we buy it here?"

"No!" was the blunt answer.

This was the only border where Bruce's presence failed to have a softening effect.

I had my revenge:

Before arresting us as poachers the Customs man was keen to extract some of the mythical benefits from the magic erection on Pythagoras's bonnet so he reached out to stroke it. Desolated to discover that it was made of hollow metal, he reacted furiously; but Bob could not suppress a choke of laughter at the ludicrous expression on the fellow's face.

24. Pythag's cheery face, and:
the funnel (with the all-important filter) which was usually over ...
... the medicine tin (that was fixed inside the spare wheel);
two spare springs bolted onto the right mudguard,
and the special toolbox on the left wing, big enough to hold essential spare parts and tools. His BC 585 number shows clearly.

Even though the sun had long since set it was out of the question to camp amongst that lot of 'gangsters' and, anyway, we had to acquire the annoying permit. So we faced the aptly named Hell Run and plunged on through the African night towards Mbeya.

It was my turn to drive and the first 35 miles were sheer nightmare. The 'highway' was littered with wrecked tankers and dotted with road works. To avoid those we had to bump off along countless long diversions. They were just *ad hoc* trails, winding through the bush, bashed out by trucks over uneven ground, across streambeds, and through woodland, shrub and savannah. We were therefore seldom on the wide, but horribly corrugated and pitted, gravel road. Naturally none of the broken-down lorries were signalled in any way. Not even one faint lantern warned of deadly dangers. Jack-knifed juggernauts sprawled across the entire track and were glimpsed only if our headlights struck some tiny area of the abandoned vehicle which wasn't thickly plastered with mud.

Bob was leaning forward in his seat looking beyond the funnel on Pythagoras's bonnet, for holes, boulders, scattered branches and – worst of all – the countless, wrecked articulated monsters. Although I drove slowly and circumspectly, time and again he yelled:

"Watch it! Something just ahead!"

We were *often* almost on top of the death trap before it became apparent. Most of the huge cylindrical tanks had punctures through which large arcs of fuel spouted (making us think of *Manneken Pis* in Brussels). The tankers' vast supplies unendingly replenished lakes of petrol that quickly evaporated or sank into the thirsty earth.

After using the famous funnel at Undro's 'brother's' pump we headed out of Mambasa in happy mood because the (now revised!) Schedule allowed us time to call at Le Station de L'Epulu that Father Laurent said was a beauty spot sited attractively on the bank of a big river.

"He told me it has a Pygmy community and some okapi and bongo" said Bob. "We haven't seen those in the game parks we've visited in previous years."

"Let's hope they're still there," I answered. "Maybe they've been eaten by guerrillas. It seems he hasn't visited Epulu for a year or two, you know. It's fifty miles away through horrible terrain, and it takes him a couple of very long days to walk there."

As we unwittingly set off into and through Ebola Territory the prospect of observing okapi and bongo excited us.

CHAPTER SIXTEEN

Kisangani bound. Pygmies.

We'd been travelling through wild territory, totally out of touch with the rest of the world. We didn't yet know that my father was fighting for his life in a Mallorcan clinic. My mother was utterly exhausted from worry, and physically worn out by having – in accordance with the then Spanish hospital custom – to attend to all the patient's physical requirements. The situation was not doing her ailing heart any good at all.

"There's a card from The Brophnes," she told her husband the morning that we left Father Laurent and his flock at Mambasa, and headed for Station de L'Epulu.

"Oh?" (Weakly). "Where are they?"

"I don't know, but they posted this from Mbeya. According to the post mark that was nine days ago."

"I hope they're getting on all right."

"Perhaps they're somewhere in the Congo by now."

"I'd like to live to see their little Bruce. That's one of my names, you know."

****

Chapter 1 told you about our visit to Station de L'Epulu.

From there, achieving the wonderful rate of 130 miles in 6 hours, we reached Nia Nia from which a right fork should have taken us to Isiro Village and then on to Central African Republic. It was disappointing when locals assured us that our proposed track had not been maintained, was without bridges, full of *grands trous,* and littered with fallen forest giants. One glance at the almost invisible start of that 'highway' confirmed those horrendous facts. Even if the trail actually continued further than round the next bend, hundreds of miles of that sort of thing was not for us. Regretfully – on our journey *northwards* to Europe – Pythagoras now had to be pointed *west-southwest*. We were lucky never to have reached Isiro Village where Ebola was festering; but our map showed alarmingly that our new route headed towards Kisangani (which we had not planned to visit) with no settlements or missions or other signs of humanity on the way. It was now 2 pm and Kisangani was 212 miles off.

Our passage across Zaire was turning out to be a like a repetitive flow chart in which we were constantly selecting the next choice. Our journey was often ordained by boxes such as:

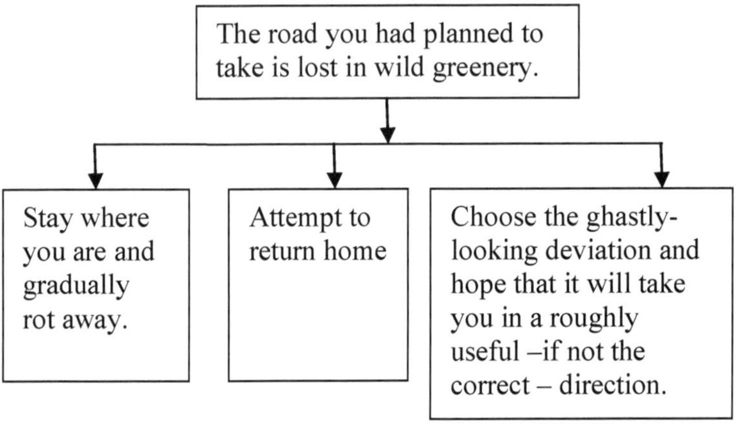
The road you had planned to take is lost in wild greenery.
Stay where you are and gradually rot away.
Attempt to return home
Choose the ghastly-looking deviation and hope that it will take you in a roughly useful –if not the correct – direction.

There really was no choice, and that was why, on Wednesday November 3rd, we found ourselves – willy nilly – in the second largest town of Zaire. Kisangani, 'city on flood's bend', was an important trade and trans-shipment centre on the Congo River, whose name implies: "Waterway that swallows all other rivers."

After Nia Nia I was thrilled to spot Pygmies for the first time on this trip. These strange people were still only just touched by civilisation where the raw road cut through their land. Whenever we caught sight of the little folk, we either stopped or rumbled very slowly towards them whispering as if they were game that we didn't want to disturb. That wasn't a bad description. They were as wary as any wild animals.

"They're wearing the scantiest of loincloths."

"Or just a bunch of leaves."

"Oh look! Some have tiny bows and arrows on their polls."

"I expect the arrows are tipped with deadly poison."

"Yes. Oh isn't it *exciting*?"

"Hm!"
"Stop, Bob. I want to take a photo."
"They're hideous. Look at their bulging pot bellies and the women's awful hanging breasts."
"Stop!"
"Surely you don't want to snap such ugly wizened creatures!"

It was unfortunate that on each of the few occasions that we came upon Pygmies by chance Bob was driving. He refused to pause near them. I don't know whether he was afraid or perhaps he had read something that he had decided wasn't fit for my ears. He just muttered:
"No time."
(Bloody Schedule!)

25. Pygmy lady intent on vanishing. Height of basket 45cm. Compare the 90cm depth of the Malawian Tea Picker's basket (picture 16 on page 36) and you'll get some idea of the Pygmies' smallness.

Meanwhile the little chaps were as much averse to seeing us as Bob was against parking to photograph them. I snatched a couple of poor shots through Pythagoras's window but the wee folk just melted nimbly and swiftly amongst the trees. One minute we saw them... the next second the jungle seemed to be completely deserted.

They were just one of the 200 ethnic groups of the vast Congo. Further north we met a tribe where brightly coloured bras must have been *le dernier cri.* (The latest fashion.) Brash and strapping women, with nothing else above their waists, marched forcefully along the track proudly displaying the obviously locally-stitched garments. Lurid orange, virulent green, startling blue, mixed psychedelic colours... all resonated against deep brown torsos. As large as the pygmies were tiny, these magnificent ladies had no need of Botox. My admiration was very slightly tinged with envy. My own 'milk factory' was working fantastically well. Bruce never went hungry; but volume-wise I could have done with a little of those buxom beauties' endowments, and actually *where* I stored the baby's sustenance was a mystery!

These Amazons were carrying brochettes of huge rats that had been split open, skewered, and then roasted by prodding the spikes into the soil round small cooking fires.

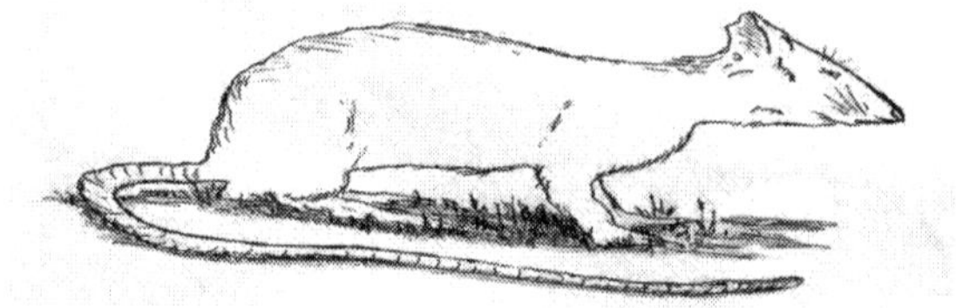

26. Another potential Ebola carrier – scrumptious when roasted.

After the last family of little people had vanished, for the rest of the day we saw no monkeys, no animals, no Pygmies, no hamlets, only myriads of butterflies and a few flocks of parrots. Neither did we spot any ordinary-sized humans except for three who gave us a real fright – as you will learn. The forest seemed to have suffocated them all.

It was hot. The road was bad. We felt extremely isolated but were grateful to find bailey bridges across several rivers. A strip of 30 miles of tar was amazing, but typically unreliable, and hence extremely stressful because of unpredictable hazards.

The track cut, as usual, through incredible stands of huge, tightly-growing bamboo and dense vegetation, which closed in below immense trees that met overhead.

There we had our second puncture of the trip. The constant battering had badly damaged the wall of another tyre. Now we had *two* dicey outers and no chance of replacing them. It was a desperately worrying situation, and the thought of later having to cross the fearsome Sahara with unreliable tyres was nothing short of petrifying.

We changed the wheel of the just-punctured tube with the one that had been patched up at Beni the day before. Although the weakness of our tyres was worrying we'd have been terribly distressed had we known that the Beni "mechanic's" excessive hammering had seriously damaged the hub. From then on Pythagoras suffered considerable pain in his rear axle and problems were brewing.

After a great many hours of plugging doggedly on, darkness and colossal trees closed in even more.

"It's high time we stopped."

"Yes. But there's absolutely nowhere to draw off the road."

We pressed forward very slowly and cautiously.

"What's that?"

"I don't... WATCH OUT! --- A crashed tanker."

"Good Heavens! It's like those juggernauts on the Hell Run, only instead of spewing fuel, a river of beer's pouring out of it."

"Crickey! It's making incredible mud as it rushes down those deep ruts."

There was no sign of the driver. Was he lying in the undergrowth having drunk himself into a coma? What a whale of a time he must have enjoyed doing so!

"Phew! What a pong!"

"Petrol (in barrels) and rattling bottles of beer seem to be the only things being transported round Zaire these days."

"More beer than fuel, I'd say".

"Yow! Careful! I'm not sure there enough space to pass."

We were longing to stop for the night.
"There's nowhere feasible to camp – not even a tiny clearing."
"And not a single miniscule settlement."
"We'll just have to grind on."

It was sheer madness to drive after dark but there really was no room for a tent anywhere. Besides, it would have been even more dangerous to camp. Vile, marauding gangs, brutalised by countless battles, wouldn't hesitate to steal all our possessions and machete us to bloody pieces. That was terrifying enough fate for us, but the image of Bruce hacked to shreds was sick making. It couldn't be risked.

It was horribly dark.
"I wish Pythagoras's headlights weren't showing this frightening tendency to die," I moaned.
"A bit of gleam from the full moon is filtering through the canopy."
"But it's not nearly enough to drive by. My eyes feel as if they're standing out on stalks with the effort of trying to peer ahead."

We saw no sign of life till twelve excessively dark miles from Kisangani a Mercedes lay at an awkward angle on the road. It was the second (deceased) sedan car we'd seen since Bukavu. In those past four and a half days we'd also counted apart from the three-Land-Rover convoy, maybe a dozen moving lorries and perhaps six immovable Land Rovers, – all in villages.

An Asian standing beside the Mercedes waved us down.
"Bandits stage apparent accidents across the road and attack when you stop."
"Don't pull up. It's dreadfully dangerous!"
"Mm. But it seems like an all-too-obvious very broken axle."
"I don't care. Keep going."
"The middle-aged gent looks utterly respectable."
"There's a shadow lurking behind the vehicle."
"What if we were stranded and passers-by just ignored us?"

Driving on a few metres, I disregarded Bob's grunt of annoyance and paused, engine in gear, my foot poised to stamp on the accelerator, ready for a rapid getaway.

CHAPTER SEVENTEEN

Stopped by night. Twelve horrendous miles.

Balancing Act.

In those few seconds while we waited our senses were pulsing from peak to peak, taut on super-stress alert. Adrenalin was pumping for instant response to whatever was about to happen. Daggers or pistols might be jammed into our ribs.

And yet I remember that, although concentrating desperately upon the fellow's advance, I was so keyed up that I noticed all sorts of irrelevant matters: the dust on the dashboard; being grateful that the baby was asleep; wondering if I could reach the machete... I felt my hair was standing on end.

An intense silence thrummed through the jungle. But it was silence only because we discounted the hundreds of noises to which we had become accustomed. All round speeding fruit bats (Ebola carriers) were emitting metallic "pings"; branches creaked; undergrowth rustled; frogs of various kinds screamed, croaked, or growled; high above us a monkey barked; probably a disturbed bird squawked briefly; far away a prowling leopard may have coughed.

The approaching footsteps dislodged stones on the track, and then suddenly the Asian was there, looking in at my window. I was expecting him, yet I jumped with fright. He explained:

"I am trembling for fear who might be attacking my party during this night. Or what animals... My daughter is with me. I am pleading you. I am begging with you to be taking her from this danger."

The lurking shadow that we'd seen behind his car turned out to be his African servant.

Disinclined to take any stranger into the car we fabricated excuses.

"What if we have an accident and your daughter's hurt?"
"We have no room for another passenger."
Then again – might she afterwards falsely accuse us of attacking her? If we were forced to stop for the night there would be plenty of space for her in the tent – always supposing that we found enough room between trees to erect it – but we had no spare airbed or bedding.

We wiggled and prevaricated.
"We are not insured to take another person." That was a lie. "Besides you can see for yourself there's no room."

Indeed, Pythagoras's so-called 'seats' were actually just a narrow metal bench sharing a common completely vertical steel back. On the bench were three very hard, small, removable squares, euphemistically called 'cushions': one for the driver – on the right – one for the passenger – on the left – and a third centrally. In front of that middle 'seat' reared the normal gear control and two extra levers, with respectively red and yellow knobs, for 4-wheel drive and for reduced gear. Anyone sitting in the middle had to knit his legs up round his ears because there really was no room for feet.
But in the end the Asian's distress was so evident that I said:
"You take over the driving, Bob. I'll curl up in the tiny centre space."

The young woman (Asha) climbed into the passenger seat avoiding the nappy bucket as much as possible. Just before we started, the man leant into our car and handed his daughter the most enormous and longest torch that either of us had ever seen – or have seen since. It had a mammoth head to match its great length. In some dialect that we could not understand he obviously told the girl to use it as a weapon should we turn nasty, or if bandits attacked us. This was noble of him, as he really needed it himself – for light and for his own defence.

Those last few miles into Kisangani were wretched with tremendous pits in the road and these became even worse once we got into town. We were praying not to succumb to another puncture. Asha, moist and shivering with fear, was constantly peering out trying to see between tremendous tree trunks or round creepers. It was difficult not to catch her terror. We were, in any case, very anxious because Pythagoras had received a severe bashing in recent days and even though nothing was evident externally strange sounds told us that he was no longer in top form mechanically. Intermittent inexplicable electric anomalies also worried us. Now, as we staggered on towards Kisangani, the headlights were dimming steadily, their power varying with the pressure on the accelerator, and we could only touch that lightly because speed was out of the question on the deeply churned-up track. Would we soon be stranded by the roadside in utter darkness?

Squashed into the central 'non-seat' my rear developed painful cramp, but at 10pm, physically and psychologically exhausted, we did finally reach Asha's home. Intense relief was mutual as she tumbled out of the car to bang on a high, corrugated iron portal. Eventually a smaller door, within the large entrance opened a crack. It was edged like the bigger gate, with uneven planks that were covered with knots similar to smallpox scabs. Vaguely we saw a very worried face peering out. Our passenger waved goodbye and was admitted. We now roamed the potholed streets searching for a hotel. I was so relieved to be free of the responsibility of Asha that I felt a tight tourniquet had been removed from my ribcage.

We dared not switch off the engine so Bob remained in Pythagoras nursing the accelerator while I went into the 3 available hotels in turn. Luckily Bruce had fallen asleep for the night many hours before and gave no sign of waking. The establishments I ventured into, probably built in the days when Russia had enjoyed a brief flirtation with the Congo, had once been splendid hotels with large reception rooms and decorative plasterwork (now cracked) edging high colonial ceilings. They were seedy, with eccentric or no plumbing, and incredible electricity problems. Our room turned out to have the luxury of an *en suite* bathroom, but that rare resource had no water!

"What about trying that stopcock."

It was high on the bathroom wall so I fetched a chair. Too wide to stand *between* any of the fittings but not wide enough to straddle bidet or loo, it didn't help us to reach the small metal wheel. Determined not to be beaten we performed a delicate balancing operation. What a pity Bruce was not of an age to appreciate or applaud the wonderful circus act that followed! We got quite expert by the end of our stay.

Two chair legs slithered about on a towel in the bidet while Bob squatted down to support the other two. I climbed onto the chair, did a poor imitation of the fairy on the Christmas tree, stretched up... and turned the stopcock. Meanwhile Bob had nearly burst a blood vessel! Magic! Water! – cold, of course. (No hotel gave us *hot* water anywhere between Mbeya, Tanganyika – and Oran, on the Mediterranean coast of Algeria.) The chilly deluge rushed out of every fawcet in bidet, basin, and bath. Not one could be closed. To flush the loo the wheel had first to be kept in the open position until the tank was full. Of course while that was happening *all* taps supplied water whether or not we wanted it. If the loo was then flushed but the stopcock left open to refill its tank we soon had a high level waterfall. Sometimes our acrobatics reduced us to helpless giggles!

With eight electricity sockets – all empty – our quarters had not a glimmer of illumination until the management reluctantly disgorged a couple of low-wattage bulbs. It was no surprise that the radio, air con, and several of the light switches, didn't function. However, room service worked. An excellent dinner was dished up stylishly with crisp tablecloth although it was then getting on for 11pm. We completed the daily chores (which included diary writing) and finally turned in at 01.00 with washed nappies festooned everywhere. The chance that Bruce would want feeding at 02.00 could not be ruled out.

In this robber–ridden zone security for Pythagoras had been my priority so I had settled on the hotel which offered a lock-up for the car: a tiny yard, enclosed by tall buildings all round, with a very lofty but narrow, corrugated iron gate, *and* a night watchman. We thought that a safe haven for the vehicle and its contents was a great blessing and probably our main need; but Kisangani had unpleasant surprises in store.

CHAPTER EIGHTEEN

In Kisangani. Albino haircut. Weighing Bruce

If Bukavu was a decayed tooth then Kisangani, which we reached after exhaustingly long and hard days, had become a moribund but still just-jerking body. Once so efficient and beautiful, now rendered shambolic by wars and hopeless administration, it was also squeezed and suffocated by incredible expanses of equatorial forest. From Bukavu to Kisangani a buzzing bluebottle, zooming in on a corpse, would fly just 282 miles. But in November 1971 we had woven a tortuous 856 miles along the only (horrid) tracks that remained.

In those 4½ days, along our very indirect and stressful course had simmered five isolated, tiny 'towns' whose dirt roads had once bustled with shops, colonial villas, corrugated iron shacks, communal water pumps, schools, dispensaries, hotels and gardens. Now those settlements, linked only by scarcely existing 'roads', were inaccessible, had no amenities and were burnt dens of potential trouble. Vegetation overwhelmed collapsing buildings that had degenerated into slums. Walls were pitted with shell and shrapnel holes. Rusting armoured cars with perished tyres lay abandoned, usually complicating empty crossroads.

When we reached Kisangani, Pythagoras and adult humans were bushed; but the wriggling scrap of humanity in the Fish Basket was in great form!

We rose early to get the car to the garage as soon as possible. The foreman seemed useless but the place was not busy and the Belgian manager was interested in our trip. He spoke a few words of English so Bob could converse with him – more or less. His wife, who spoke only French, was fascinated by Bruce and shocked that we had no idea of his weight. With a dismissive wave of a well-rounded hand she insisted:
"Come. Abandon the men to gaze like idiots into the entrails of your car. Let them succour it if they can. I know an Indian grocer who has scales where we shall weigh the baby."

It was a sweaty business walking through the drizzle-damned, almost empty streets of Kisangani, which should have been a thriving city, rumbling with all sorts of vehicles and raucous pedestrians. Only lackadaisical people slouched past without apparent desire to reach any destinations. A barber's small, folding table wobbled on an uneven, stone-and-slush pavement. Under a sagging 'roof' of patched plastic material, an albino with blotchy caramel-brown and livid-white skin was having his enormous shock of hair chopped. He blinked white eyelashes over pink eyes at each decisive click of the scissors. Judging by the length of the thick mat this must have been an annual event and the barber was operating like a harvester attacking a field of corn. Places where the machine had not yet passed stood up a good 5 inches from the head like tall woodland surrounded by grazed fields. Frizzy, yellowish-white tufts drifted in puddles, and lay scattered among cracked, bare toes of watchers who in other African countries would have been bubbling with comments and conversation. Here there was no cheery chatter, just silence and stony stares. Off the torn 'waterproof' sheeting rivulets of rain dripped dismally.

In the Asian's shop, to the joy of a small crowd of onlookers, we balanced the squirming and uncooperative baby, in the manner of a bag of potatoes, upon the merchant's very basic weighing device. I only knew Bruce's birth weight in lbs, so much discussion and scratching of heads was needed to convert the shopkeeper's kilograms to British Units. Scribbling on my palm with a wobbly biro, I eventually deduced that Bruce had put on 26 ounces since leaving Blantyre. I had no idea whether this called for celebration or moans, but Madame was devastated. She couldn't imagine what 26 ounces signified!

After 'tattooing' my hand with a lot more computations, 26 oz were converted into grams and Madame declared herself delighted. I could therefore be happy though I had my doubts about the margin of error produced by the extraordinary scales and my laborious arithmetic. Don't ask why I hadn't changed the birth weight into metric units in the first place! That would have saved one set of calculations, but the onlookers would have been deprived of much hilarity!

Madame and I returned to the garage.
"How're you getting on?" we asked.
"Thanks to the manager's supervision Pythagoras has received prompt attention," said Bob. "The headlight anomaly has been cured by adjusting the voltage regulator." (Which caused grief later!) "Thick sediment was bunging up the carburettor – despite all our best efforts with the petrol filter! That and the fuse box are now clean."

No one could solve the mystery of why the fan occasionally caused short-circuiting but this was a precursor of utterly amazing things to come. While Bob continued to supervise work on Pythagoras, I left Bruce sleeping in his basket – undisturbed by mechanics banging doors and clattering tools.
"You're not to let anyone move his mosquito net," I ordered in harridan tones. I knew Bob wouldn't budge from the car because the luggage had to be guarded.

Intending to change Travellers' Cheques I naturally sought the Bank, but was startled to be told:
"*Mais Madame*, foreign currency matters are dealt with only in Kinshasa – the capital."
A Scottish missionary indicated a shop
"*They*'ll change your cheques," she said. "But the rate's ruinous."
She was right. (Might she have been the sister mentioned on page 6 by one of the Blantyre Club's pessimistic 'Codgers'?) The garage also converted some cheques – at an even more horrifying rate! The manager explained:
"I receive more money by sending your cheques to Belgium. And that way I will obtain it sooner than if I deal with Kinshasa."

We ate a picnic lunch beside the Congo River. Its muddy banks were spectacularly littered.
"Gracious! How filthy everything is. The water's absolutely *disgusting*!"
"That's why everyone filters and then boils the city supply for *ages* before using it."
"The river's not even a quarter as wide as the Zambezi that we cross so regularly on that awful Tête pontoon in Mozambique."

Tied to the bank were enormously long dugouts.
"They're like the one that Mother (a scant 5 foot in her socks!) and I took in 1943," I told Bob, "when we did the Cape to Cairo overland. Having been evacuated from Egypt to South Africa because Rommel's guns could be heard from Alexandria we were then stuck in a very beautiful and varied country; but we wanted to be at home, in Egypt. Because of the war there were no boats or planes available to civilians. So we went by land."
"Wow!" said Bob. "Wasn't that a bit drastic?"
"I suppose it was, even though Congolese conditions in 1943 were infinitely better then than they are now. We travelled by train to Elizabethville, arranged a 3-day taxi drive through the equatorial forest, and went *up the Congo* River on canoes like these. But this lot are propelled by outboard motors: not nearly so romantic as the paddlers of earlier years. Once out of the Congo into the Sudan we travelled by native bus."
"See those riverboats," I went on.
"Obviously not designed for rough waters," scorned Bob looking at an old sternwheeler and a high-decked passenger vessel. "They'd never survive the turbulent Zambezi waters."

27. On the Congo River.
(The extra-long dugouts with engines are not shown.)

"But on our journey when I was 6 years old, Mother and I went *down the Nile* for a week on a paddle steamer just like those."
"Then you're damn lucky the crocs didn't get you. That's all I can say!"

We delivered the letter entrusted to us by the Mbeya émigrés. The recipients quickly wrote a reply and asked:
"Please post that if you ever get outside Zaire. You'll come to supper won't you?" We declined their invitation because we had been advised to leave Kisangani at 4am the next day and they confirmed what other locals had warned:
"The road to Buta is so abominable that even powerful lorries and 4X4 vehicles pass only with immense difficulty."

What a jolly prospect! And there was no chance of even one sunny hour to alleviate the situation. For the past few days clouds had hovered unremittingly. Daylight didn't pour down as it does in other parts of Africa. Instead a yellow-blue bruise colour seemed to be smeared everywhere. In the jungle this was understandable because the light was filtered through countless leaves and blocked by branches. There was an all-pervading smell of dampness. Here in Kisangani even though huge trees were being kept at bay by ramshackle houses, the green atmosphere still predominated and the overall stench was of unclean moisture. Clouds apparently trapped under an inverted bowl, stayed squatting over us like feathers of a brooding evil spirit. The misty evenings chilled our bones, but Bob found Kisangani's daytime humid heat unbearable, so promising to 'watch' Bruce while I sought postcards, he crashed out and slept for 2 hours. Luckily, after the 'excitement' (?!) of not falling off the grocer's scales the baby emulated his father.

I had a long walk to find a shop with cards. That and no queues in the post office were signs of the degeneration of business and total breakdown of the tourist trade. Along our route we sent missives to our parents from any apparently functioning mail centre that we came across. (The one before this had been in Bujumbura in Burundi.) In this age of electronic miracles it seems incomprehensible that postal efforts were our only means of making contact. We didn't know that the cards, pinned to a map of Africa on the wall of Father's hospital room, showed our progress up the continent, and cheered my anxious parents.

In the evening we were surprised to find that Asha's father had bothered to trace us. The actual details of such a search were simple: there were only three possible hotels to visit and no other families were mad enough to travel through the Congo. He and his son insisted on buying us a drink in the hotel bar where blissful air-conditioning was actually working. We felt uncomfortable because we had accepted the young woman so unwillingly, but the atmosphere thawed and they joined us for supper. Our plans for a rapid meal and an early night were thus upset.

The gentleman was a big wheel who owned a rice mill and a chain of stores throughout this vast country, plus a branch office in Kampala. He was an interesting person with a fund of information, theories about the state of Zaire, and entertaining stories which he recounted with verve and humour. Unfortunately the dinner, though most enjoyable, delayed our preparations for a very early start the next day; but, irredeemably optimistic, we checked out of the hotel that evening hoping to get away promptly in the morning.

28. The excitements of weighing Bruce.

CHAPTER NINETEEN

<u>Thieves. Ploughing through chocolate cake.</u>

(In this Chapter you may want to refer to the picture on page 85 of Pythagoras's cheery face.)

During the night an almighty thunderstorm exploded. Lashing rain boded ill for the state of the reputedly appalling track out of Kisangani. When, the next morning, dodging downpour and swirling puddles, I went down to get clean nappies from the car I was shocked to the marrow:
'Our medicine tin! The lid's all bent up! What's happened? Oh – NO! There's nothing in it! All our remedies that Dr Hart in Blantyre advised me about so carefully – all *gone*! Oh my God!'

Our 'drugs locker' was an empty biscuit tin that fitted cosily within the hub of the spare wheel on Pythagoras's bonnet. It was kept there by a system that included a padlock and foam padding, the latter to minimise jolts and to keep the contents cool – we hoped! It was a patent idea of which I had been very proud, unjustifiably so as it turned out. One of its advantages was that it was easily available. The thieves appreciated this ease of access! The lock was still firmly closed so the robbers agreed that the impressive padlock was not one to be removed illegally. They showed, however, that without needing a key they could prise up the lid and extract every single item! Disaster! In this land of awful insects and appalling diseases, where accidents lurked beyond every rut, how would we manage without our medical kit?

Well, that was gone. Was anything else missing? Frantically I checked the big steel toolbox that we'd had welded onto Pythagoras's left wing. Its two padlocks had not been broken. The special tools and imported spare parts were still inside. Phew! The two new springs were still firmly riveted on the right wing. Phew again!

Pythagoras's 'rhino horn'? – That would surely attract a thief. We kept it outside the car because it smelt of petrol and, being dangerously pointed, it was awkward to pack. Where was the funnel? I groaned with relief when I remembered that in towns we always carried it inside the vehicle. It was too easily removed and too fascinating to risk on the bonnet in its normal position. Checking inside Pythag I breathed a little more easily. Nothing had gone. But the loss of all our medicines was too awful to take in.

The night guard had vanished.

"But I gave him six Zaire last night," moaned Bob bitterly. In those days that was a big sum. "And I promised ten more if the vehicle was still OK by morning."

"Obviously he decided that selling pills, bandages, syringes, lotions etc would be more profitable than the promised second generous tip or keeping his job."

"We're in *dire* straits now!"

"I'm sure we won't be able to get replacements."

"The cost is bound to be outrageous, too."

The darkest waves of depression and fury engulfed us.

Later, when Bob drove Pythagoras round to the hotel entrance, he appeared looking grim: "Windscreen wipers, indicators and interior lights are all on strike!"

My heart shrivelled into a hard little ball and plummeted. These faults might indicate something much more serious and a dysfunctional vehicle could mean disaster. I always panicked if the car developed ailments when we were travelling.

Although outraged with the garage we were actually extremely fortunate because: first, had it not been raining we wouldn't have tried the windscreen wipers till we were once again beyond help, and secondly, when the bad work was repaired (for nothing) the workshop manager heard about the theft and took us to his friend, the director of a pharmaceutical company, who very kindly replaced – free of charge – some of the items that had vanished.

Returning to the hotel we accosted the (Belgian) manager who was extremely polite and regretful.

"Whatever you do, don't report your loss to the police. Instead of hunting for the thief they'll surely arrest *you,* and that will be the last we'll ever hear of you," he advised. Handing us a requisition form he added: "Here is a 'permit' to buy everything you need on the hotel's account, from the town's biggest pharmacy."

We found substitutes for as many of the not-yet-replaced medicines as we could remember. The snakebite kit was not as complete as our original outfit and inevitably we later regretted having forgotten to replace some essentials. The various people who helped us to re-equip explained that businesses had all been nationalised so they had no more interest in financial outcomes but their kindness was nevertheless much appreciated.

Everyone warned us that we faced a region where the going was ghastly. They were right; but they forgot to mention that there'd inevitably be hilarious episodes! What we *didn't* anticipate, despite what we'd been told, was how many scary rivers and swamps we'd have to cross on horrifyingly derelict pontoons.

But what were we to do? There was nothing to induce us to remain in the isolated town of mildewed houses where all enterprise was stifled by suffocating governmental bureaucracy; and it was out of the question to fly the rest of the way, abandoning Pythagoras and 99% our belongings. We'd set out to drive to Europe; so that had to be achieved. We climbed into the Land Rover.

All the palaver with the garage and acquiring new medical stocks took time so it was not till midday that we finally turned north and half joyfully, half consumed with apprehension, started on the second part of our efforts to plough across Zaire. It took us another $5^1/_2$ laborious days to reach the end of our Congo epic; but at least we were now grinding along more or less northwards, *towards* our ultimate goal and not away from it.

The pelting rain had to our immense relief lessened when, bucketing painfully over potholes, we left the drenched, smelly and subdued streets of Kisangani. I pondered:

'When we headed away from Bukavu we were unwise and inexperienced. Now, after $4^{1}/_{2}$ days rumbling through Zaire's *partially* functioning eastern Kivu Province and then crossing the incredibly unpopulated and unbelievably dense equatorial forest we've learnt a lot. In the almost sinking 'island' of Kisangani, we reached a place with at least a semblance of civilised life. Are we mad to drive away from that haven of relative safety?'

The first 57 miles of road were absolutely terrible. Imagine hilly terrain made of bottomless, soft, chocolate cake full of treacherous rocks and liberally coated with thick unset icing...

Knee-deep mud. VISCOUS! – Clinging.

Slime – STENCH! Prolonged squelches as our tyres strain to turn. Pythagoras roars with the effort of battling through churned-up filth. Water pours down the middle of the track. Small rivers rush on each side. When we are not skidding round through 180° – and back again – progress is painfully slow. Slither – skate – squish.

Terrified of leeches and cut feet, I hitch my skirt well above my knees and wade through slushy depths of unavoidable minor lakes. I feel about with my toes. Slosh! Seek the least treacherous route for Pythagoras to follow. Slip. The stinking muck is unbearable, but has to be suffered. The engine growls.

We mustn't go skidding away, plunging among the big trees, bouncing off massive trunks. We daren't let Pythag's wheels shimmy into any deep lorry tracks. That would be fatal. We'd be stranded with our belly on the central ridge of slime and our wheels in the air.

The horrible sensation of sliding helplessly is devastating. I wave frantically.

"This way! Don't stall whatever happens. Keep one wheel on the middle spine."

Progress is desperately slow.

A misunderstood signal! We're stuck – axle deep in glutinous sludge.

"Get the spade."

It's in a rubber bag, made from an old inner tube, chained and padlocked onto the back of the Land Rover together with the Hi-lift jack and the long handle of the little jack. Find keys. Undo padlocks and mud-coated chains that hold the revolting, slime-encrusted bundle in place. Clumsy work.

'Please God we don't have to use the mud/sand tracks! They're so massive and ungainly – so tedious to handle – such an effort to unshackle them and heave them off the roof – so heavy to lift back up ... and if, with their help, we manage to battle out of the mire's clutches, while we shove them back onto the rack, Pythagoras will have to be stationary – sinking – getting more stuck again...'

Numerous long-abandoned, rusting and broken trucks lying at all angles in the mire testify to the horrors of these miles, so men, eager to earn a few small coins, are not far away. We are observed. A boy emerges from the surrounding jumble of green. He stares, pauses and yells. Soon a small army surrounds us. No shouting and laughing. No contradictory instructions screamed from all sides. NO. This is Zaire where people are sullen and almost silent. This lot speak little but they push effectively. An enormous and time-consuming effort – much digging... We're coated all over in disgusting ooze – and exhausted!

A l—o—n—g shove ... Slowly – slowly... We start to move, slew round, make headway ... The helpers jog beside us to receive through the window bonus sweets and the agreed sum, equivalent to about 6/-, in small coins. We're away...

Flashes of colourful parrots in the canopy high overhead. No opportunity to admire them. Keep your eyes on the quagmire. Avoid those deep holes if you can – try to go round that huge rock...

Another lorry on its side – taking up almost all the track. This juggernaut's driver is still with his vehicle – unusual. He's signalling us to stop. We daren't. No room anyway to take that burly fellow aboard. He looks really evil, too. Besides – we can't assist such a huge tanker. Don't lose Pythag's revs. Keep moving at all costs. Try not to skid into the truck. Can we miss the spewed beer bottles? Avoid the sharp scattered shards of glass.

Snarling loudly, still in four-wheel drive and reduced second gear, Pythagoras just made it through yet another long uphill expanse of the most fearful bog – again with another shattered behemoth stuck in the middle. But what an effort! The deep goo sometimes clutched our tyres as though it would never release them and at other moments sent us into terrifying spins with ravines and ditches avoided by a hairsbreadth. The steering wheel was like a thing alive. Wrestling with it tied Bob's arms practically into spirals! After our brief spell on the deeply pockmarked but still just passable city roads of Kisangani, we now knew that we were back on the infamous trans-Africa 'highway'!

Strangely after this traumatic stretch we seemed to acquire a kind of "Stockholm Syndrome" towards Congolese conditions. Before reaching Kisangani the jungle, the terrain, the people had seemed scary. We had left the wonderful wide veldt and savannah of South and East Africa that we knew so well. We no longer had glorious ochre views of rolling grasses and blue-grey mountain ridges folding away apparently into infinity... Instead we had plunged, as if through seaweed, into murky forest where it always seemed to be drizzling.

Nothing changed materially after Kisangani, but our attitude slowly altered. Like many Africans we came to 'just accept' whatever befell, and without anything actually being said there was a feeling in Pythagoras that nothing was left to us but to push on--- and on--- and on---

CHAPTER TWENTY

Ferries. Leopard and monkeys.

It would have been sensible to stop at the sleepy administrative centre of Banali that we reached soon after 5pm. We'd have had the tent up and I could have washed nappies, prepared tomorrow's lunch and cooked supper all before sunset. But there was nobody at Banali able to repair the puncture, which had occurred when a steel-like stem of elephant grass pierced an outer casing and went straight on through the inner tube. The Mission was 'dead' and the 'hotel' swarmed with prostitutes in frightening states of inebriation, so we decided to press on for a further 15 miles to where rumour said there might be a Protestant Mission.

We found our way barred by the Aruwimi River that Pythagoras could not, as usual, splash through by bouncing from boulder to boulder. Here we found the first of many pontoons. Most of the original ferries over the rivers had lost propellers, dropped engines into the deep, or otherwise come to grief. A funnel on a muddy bank here... a paddlewheel in the shallows elsewhere... testified to long extinct glories. Two boats had been bombed, leaving only midstream wrecks. Defunct craft could be seen corroding among well-established reeds. Instead, men pulling on cables, if you were lucky, or else yanking on fraying ropes of twisted local creepers, hauled makeshift rafts across murky waters.

Compared to the ferries that we experienced later, the first pontoon (after Banali) was very superior because it was relatively large and it still had an engine. Unfortunately it languished on the far bank. We hooted Pythagoras's horn and waited, observing from a distance the unprepossessing craft on which we hoped to cross the river.

"Its motor's mounted on one of four small launches. It doesn't look to me as if they're lashed together very firmly."

"At least it's got a sort of platform of planks."
"But all its bits are obviously in an advanced state of decay.
"So what's new? Have you spotted *anything* in Zaire that isn't about to collapse or else totally smashed?"
"We shouldn't have to wait so long. Hoot again."
When the ferrymen eventually appeared they tried hard to make us pay an extra fee for forcing them to work after hours.
"It wouldn't be 'after hours', you rogues, if you hadn't taken so long to turn up."
Luckily they didn't understand English!

The dreadfully sozzled 'captain' horrified us, but later familiarity with that sort of unpleasantness, and with long waits while hastily 'press-ganged' men shambled up for work, bred a disregard, which in retrospect was amazing. But it wouldn't have done the slightest good to have expected better service.

When enough men had finally assembled and brought the raft across to our side of the river, we saw muscular individuals lifting what looked like massive, tree trunks split-lengthwise. They positioned several of these, flat side down, for us to drive up onto the rickety 'boat'.
"Good Heavens!" exclaimed Bob. "Those fellows must be terribly strong! Look how they're handling the huge logs!"
The lifters of logs noticed our admiration and grinned as if at a huge joke. The explanation was simple. The half tree trunks were more or less hollow – eaten empty by termites. So the timbers put down as a loading ramp splintered and broke as we drove aboard. The pieces were swept away like matchsticks on the current. Luckily Pythagoras didn't leave his rear dangling in the water!

Goodness knows how long that wood had been lying unused in the long grass. Even mail services had been abandoned. The Kisangani Post Office asked us to deliver along the route letters to various missions and settlements that *they* optimistically believed might still be functioning and which *we* unjustifiably hoped would provide somewhere to camp.

The 'captain' downed the last of the beer that he had been clutching to his chest, cast the bottle into the flood, and suddenly crumpled onto the 'deck', face-downwards in a puddle. His crew exploded into raucous laughter. One of the men grabbed his arm and another provoked a ripping sound as he yanked at the seat of the captain's tattered shorts. Heaving their boss roughly out of the water they dumped him on his back, spread-eagled, mouth agape and snuffling.

When we were halfway across Bob and I suddenly turned to each other with the same question: "Without the now disintegrated and therefore non-existent ramp how are we going to drive off onto the further bank?"

"*Attendez*!" ordered the boatmen. ("Wait!") Before abandoning the captain to stentorian slumbers one of them filled a rusty bailing tin with cloudy river water and emptied it into the captain's crotch. This again caused convulsive merriment! We hadn't expected to be entertained by slapstick humour. That was a bonus!

Leaving us stranded on the pontoon, with a couple of men up to their thighs in dark brown swirls to stop us being washed away, the rest, still howling with all-consuming mirth, dived into the jungle brandishing machetes, and soon re-emerged carrying strong bamboo poles. These they chopped to suitable lengths to replace the rotted tree trunks; but we were not consoled and pointed out that bamboo, being round, might roll sideways and escape from under our tyres. We would be left with wheels in mid air – or worse – in the river. The men nodded morosely to acknowledge this problem; but they were only temporarily stymied. Soon they had collected enough lianas to tie the poles together – at least for the time being.

To be honest in view of the lack of traffic it was incredible that ferries operated at all. And since they were universally on their last legs it was amazing that we suffered no accidents when we used them.

The road now became tunnel-like: extremely narrow and hemmed in at top and sides by very thick growth, yet we reached the Protestant Mission that was our objective without major trouble. Although the African pastor was away his flock made us so welcome that they wanted us to sleep in one of their own little houses. We declined their kind invitation because the last thing we wanted was to inconvenience anyone.

As we prepared to pitch the tent among 5 or 6 hovels, the creaking, rustling, 'silence' of the ever-moving jungle was shattered by high drama in surrounding giant trees. My hair stood on end as a blood-freezing explosion of high-pitched shrieks conveyed panic-stricken fury and fear. I managed a petrified squeak:

"What's that terrible noise?"

A woman sitting on the ground outside her hut and nonchalantly chopping leaves for supper heard my frightened whisper.

"Only a leopard hunting monkeys."

Her tone was disparaging.

"Of course," she seemed to imply, "everyone knows that!"

Thuds of leaping bodies made enormous spreads of canopy crash about madly... Deep reverberating grunts from the huge cat... cascading twigs... all sounded close but in fact must have been some distance away.

The racket conveyed the scene vividly: screaming monkeys with terrified eyes fleeing ever higher into thinning branches where the heavier predator dared not follow. We heard vicious spits, and bark being torn with dagger-like claws as, forced to let its prey escape, the huge cat scrambled furiously down to the forest floor, presumably backwards in the manner of a domestic cat.

"Is the leopard not afraid of humans?" I asked the woman. She shrugged, but with an averted head, so maybe fear was mutual.

CHAPTER TWENTY ONE

Buta 'hotel'. Soldiers. Short of water,

Midnight homicide?

As we covered 109 miles in 5.5 hours and reached Buta after lunch, a rock gave us a particularly vicious wallop. Bob and I were shaking with shock but Bruce was unfazed. He just grabbed harder with his toothless gums, inevitably swallowing wind. (Stocking up fuel for a later tantrum!) Luggage in the back of Pythagoras was upturned and in chaos. Nothing very unusual in that, but stopping to put things right, we were horrified to discover a flood cascading fast from under the rear door.

Panic!

"Oh GODFATHERS! What's *happened*?"

Apart from doing less drastic damage, the stupendous bump had caused our *full* (and therefore very heavy) 25 litre, water container made of thick, re-enforced plastic to bounce so unbelievably that one lower corner was smashed – to tiny pieces – far beyond gluing together. Frantically we turned the jerry can sideways to put the hole uppermost.

"O.M.G! We've got only about two litres left!"

"How are we to replace what we've lost?"

"Heaven knows! We obviously can't use the rivers even though there are so many of them."

"Goodness no! The people round here have frightful goitres."

The great hanging growths were disgusting and disfiguring. At the time we believed (erroneously) that these develop from a waterborne disease.

"The streams will also be full of dysentery, typhoid and bilharzias." Bob seemed to be taking a perverse joy in the list!

"Of course. And liquid sold as 'water' by the prostitutes' 'bars' is foul. It would definitely make us ill."

"How on earth did we forget such a *vital* item as Water Purifying Tablets after the Kisangani theft?"

To exacerbate our water problems, ever since the Kisangani mechanic had adjusted the regulator, Pythagoras's battery fluid had been evaporating amazingly. We'd run out of distilled water so we had to top up the battery – often – with drinking water boiled and then filtered (through Bob's handkerchief). Now we had scarcely any of that. Bob decided that it would be "Beer for breakfast" but I can never drink more than a couple of mouthfuls of the stuff and how would Bruce's digestion react to a diet of fermented maize – and all the other unpleasant 'thickening' bits that went into the local "Primus Beer"? He already excelled at volcano-like burps. One 4am eruption had even startled into amazed consciousness a deeply-sleeping Bob – who now joked:

"It'll give him an excuse to explain when he's grown up: – Well, you see, I'm an alcoholic because my mother had to drink the Zairian Primus brew when I was a baby."

The name of that revolting concoction fascinated us. Was it somehow incredibly linked to Latin and meant to imply 'The best quality'? Or were people so dazzled by the efficacy of Primus Stoves (when they worked, and when paraffin to fuel them could be obtained) that they had named a beer after those dangerous cookers?

Buta was beautifully situated on the loop in a tributary of the Congo River. Because it contained an army barracks, and had once been on the (now defunct) railway to Isiro, it was slightly bigger than most hamlets. Perhaps it was still an administrative hub but without the railway it was probably no longer a mining centre. Otherwise it was a typical settlement to be found in any jungle clearing, notable mostly for raucous prostitutes sheathed in yards of dirty satinised drapery and usually drunk. From the brothel, euphemistically called a 'Bar', deafening 'music' assaulted the surrounding jungle. Electricity came from thumping generators – which worked when diesel was available. I split my sides laughing at the horrified glare and utter panic of my 'Oh-so- correct' spouse as he parried amorous advances of a 'wanna-be beauty'. Luckily she accepted the rebuff with fatalistic equanimity, and directing a belittling shrug at him, staggered off.

Our first priority, on reaching the small, straggling village was to find the puncture repairman whose workshop was in the local barracks. We watched as intently as hungry jackals trying to steal a bite from a lions' kill as, using our kit of course, the friendly but incompetent fellow achieved his job with much unnecessary hammering. He took so long that soldiers started and finished a football match before the repaired wheel was back on Pythagoras's back door. It was then too late to risk trying to escape the importuning whores by plugging on to an unspecifiable destination so we pitched camp in the dubious safety of a mud patch in front of the 'hotel'.

The Minister for Finance had built the place only 4 years previously and as designed it must have been really alluring. However, the air-conditioning no longer functioned, hot water had never been installed, the plumbing was fictional (causing surrounding plants to die through irrigation with excess ammonia!), no meals were provided, and nothing except 'Primus beer' was sold in the bar. It was run by the usual bevy of 'professional ' women and was in a state of general disrepair almost equal to theirs

31. Hippo wading out to graze on land.

The nearby river formed a wonderful background with splashing hippos adding to the atmosphere with their deep 'belly laughs'. That evocative sound of African waterways, and the mewing shriek of African Fish Eagles delighted us and also made us homesick for Malawi. Dramatically throwing back their heads till snowy crowns nearly touched their splendid russet shoulders, those grand birds echoed each other's yells across the river. In that delightful, glittering avian paradise we spotted spoonbill storks, pelicans, various forms of ibis, fantastic colours of different bee-eaters, little blue waxbills, and hosts of other twittering, fluttering, wading, fish-catching, and insect snatching friends.

1. Spoonbill. (About 1m tall.) (Red bill and legs.)

While I completed jobs in the tent and car, and put Bruce to 'bed' in his Fish Basket, Bob absorbed some 'local colour' by chatting with three African teachers who worked at a nearby (still functioning) Norwegian Protestant Mission. We'd have tried to reach that had we known it existed. They told him

about Zaire's educational system and how it was organising its own school-leaving certificates. They also said:
"There's a lot of mixed game here, but it quickly vanishes."

We did regularly spot signs that the jungle teemed with animals; but sadly, though the *wildlife* probably observed *us*, *we* usually missed *it*, partly because the fauna disappeared immediately, but mostly because we were fixated on the track. Besides, our two-score and more rattling padlocks and the equipment-securing chains made such a DIN that animals probably took fright long before we were anywhere near them. Insects, however, sometimes *compelled* us to notice them.

"I wish I knew more about creepy crawlies," I moaned one day as I persuaded a magnificent beetle to leave the car.
"That's a splendid specimen you've got there. He's huge!"
"Remember the beauties in Goma?"
"Oh yes! Striking things with both red and yellow stripes, like phantasmagorical humbugs."
"They were 'bugs' all right but not the sweetie kind. That type of brightly-coloured insect usually has a vile taste."
"Mm. To disgust predators."
"I really liked the horribly bilious-looking beasties with yellow blotches."
"Yeah and they were iridescent too. Absolutely amazing!"

Spectacular for their stripes, spots, brilliance and claw-like antennae, creatures that seemed to have just crawled out of frightening fairy stories, staggered across roads, through vegetation, over our food and into the tent. As we prepared for bed in Buta, Bob asked in a hollow voice:
"What do you think *that* is?"
My eyes followed his pointing finger and I jumped with fright. Taking a hasty pace backwards I stepped on a tube of toothpaste. It burst phenomenally! Inevitably we trod the stuff everywhere before I had time to clean up the mess the next morning. At least it smelled nice.

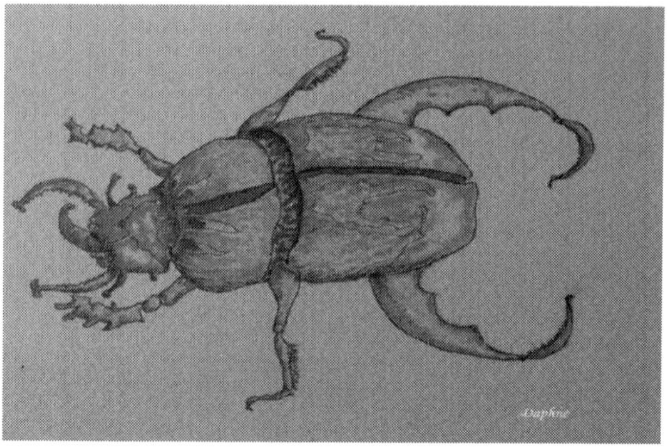

30. The Buta beetle, from inflamed memory!

On the tent wall was creeping the most grotesque black shape. Then we both laughed – rather shakily! – as we realised that some quirk of light had produced a magnified shadow of what was presumably a very dull creature. Investigation revealed however, that it was a hand-sized, iridescent green beetle sporting red under its wings and with extraordinary jaws. He was also determined to commit suicide by flying into our paraffin lamp. Despite his splendours we threw him out and inhospitably re-zipped the tent door.

A tidal wave of unmannerly and alarmingly armed soldiers suddenly swarmed into and around the hotel. They frightened us as they strutted about shouting, and blatantly carried on with the women in ways that shocked and disgusted us. Several times Bob muttered

"We'd better strike camp and sleep in the car."

We didn't; but we spent several hours very much on the *qui vive*. Perhaps reflecting our anxiety, Bruce threw a paddy the next morning so cooking breakfast had to be a juggling act.

At suppertime primeval forest had hummed all round, bitingly wet and cold. As usual constant twanging of tree frogs 'plinked' madly as if a thousand children equipped with high-pitched tin clickers from Christmas crackers were operating frantically amid the dripping foliage. Often choruses of bigger varieties in rivers/ponds provided lullabies, and sometimes bullfrogs made the air vibrate with deep-throated roaring. All the squeaking, croaking, booming... made no impression because they were common African sounds. When, at the age of fourteen, I was sent from Ethiopia to boarding school in Britain, more than anything else I missed the happily rejoicing frogs. Zairian nights were usually also busy with birdcalls, bat squeaks, creaking insects and the occasional grunts or shrieks of larger nocturnal creatures. Those were all friendly noises. It was the unusual yells of the sex-orgy soldiers and piercing screeches from their incredibly co-operative women that petrified us.

Those disturbances stopped eventually. Later, in the darkest hour soft 'small animal' sounds woke me. On autopilot I found my torch and scrambled from sleeping bag onto my knees. The Brat's revving-up noises faltered as he felt me removing his wet nappy. I lobbed it into the pail, and before he could wind himself up into full war cry, held him to my breast. With a satisfied grunt he eagerly clamped on for his predawn suck.

For once it seemed that everything, from trees to rain, was holding its breath. Hippos were probably on land, grazing, so even they weren't snorting. Unusual silence pressed, and liberated unwanted thoughts.

'What if one day we just can't go on?

Supposing we break an axle, or one of us falls ill. What if we can't obtain fuel?'

It could be weeks before any vehicle passed. Medical centres were days apart and even when reached, were of frightening quality, desperately lacking in equipment, staff and medicines. Before plunging into Africa's 'solar plexus region' we simply hadn't realised the dangers. They were beyond imagination. The deadly insects, venomous reptiles, murderous tribes, unpleasant drunks, all-engulfing vegetation, endless downpours and impossible 'roads' had to be experienced to be appreciated. It was the stuff of nightmares.

Bruce came up for air and one of his famous burps, so I transferred him to the second breast and changed to more comfortable thoughts: we'd been made happy by fantastic views, wonderful butterflies, astounding flowers, friendly people, unbelievable experiences... There'd been plenty of laughs... Pythagoras was giving signs of wear but still plugging on... We were healthy and had much for which to be grateful.

Having again patted up the baby's wind, I replaced him in the Fish Basket, fitted a clean nappy, carefully arranged the net and still on autopilot, fell once more into exhausted sleep. But it didn't last!

Suddenly terrifying screams split the night. I shot up into sitting position grasping the big hammer automatically. Even Bob, the most gifted sleeper, woke, visibly shaking with fright. With terrified eyes he opened his mouth but no sound emerged. Surely an utterly horrendous, bloodthirsty murder was being committed just outside the tent! Ear-splitting shrieks paralysed us. A victim was in agony... Would we be next? Should we dare to intervene? But after a few tense seconds of comprehensive funk we both released our held breaths with huge gusts of relief.

"Oh gosh! Only a Bush Baby! Why do such tiny creatures make such hellish noises?"

Also known as Night Apes they are fluffy but pugnacious little beasties with huge eyes, bushy tails, and ears that can be wiggled a 'thousand' ways independently like a chameleon's eyes.

"Janet, my neighbour in Rhodesia, had a tame Bush Baby called *Pookey,*" I said trying to deflate the tension that had electrified our tent.

"I know," said Bob as he settled back into his sleeping bag. "Unfortunately the 'sweet' wee monsters pee on their paws to make it easier to grab branches (or, in the case of pets – curtains!). As far as I'm, concerned that's the final straw."

Unconsciously he rubbed his hands on his sleeping bag sheet as if to clean his paws.

"I'd just as soon the little dears stayed in the forest. Besides, who'd want one yelling blue murder in the house every night – eh? Jan must've been mad!"

32. A Large Galago. (Note the claw.)

Night Apes are primates properly referred to as 'Galagos' but they are often called 'Bush Babies' because some of their yells sound like screaming infants. They are very vocal and produce a great variety of weird and strident sounds which have provoked strange superstitions. One of these is the belief that the Bush Babies' extraordinary 'chortles' come from an eerie giant snake with a feathered head. To see this reptile means certain death: a fable that, of course, can't be checked!

The sketch on the previous page shows a 'Large Galago'. Endowed with pale yellow eyelids, these deceptively charming little creatures look as if they're wearing stage eye shadow.

Bush Babies in general have ten flat nails but the Large variety (as opposed to various smaller species) has a noticeable claw on both 'first fingers'. Large Galagos grow to about 26 inches from head to the end of an ample 12-inch tail. Their woolly fur is grey with longer black hairs while the face, crown, nape and down middle of the back can be yellowish-brown. They often have a rusty tinge to the under parts and tail. Need I add: They are 'nocturnal'?

Bush Babies can protect their ears by folding them right down close to their heads. They are alcoholics, fond of fermenting fruit on which they sometimes get 'drunk', and tame Galagos can take two or three days to sleep off their potations if they get at their owners' booze! When cunning Pookey, outwitted Jan's teetotalling controls his hangovers could be hilarious!

Deadly foe!

CHAPTER TWENTY TWO

A terrible loss. Bitten – but by *what?*

Now we desperately needed water. That was frantic enough, but another great problem was to hit us during the coming morning. It was the worst disaster of our whole 13,487-mile Trans-Africa-and-Europe trip.

At the time in Kenya nearly all 4X4s had a Hi-lift jack. We went to much trouble to import into Malawi one of these huge but then little-known instruments. If properly used a Hi-lift raises the car to incredible heights with only a few easy pulls on a lever and, later, lowers the vehicle quickly without any jerk. In those days the Land Rover Company supplied a toy-like jack that had to be carefully positioned and then operated by turning a long, difficult-to-manage, remote-control-sort-of handle. On flat, horizontal and hard surfaces these little devices were just about adequate, though tedious to manipulate. On irregular mushy roads we found such a gimmick was almost worthless.

In case it ever *had* to be used we carried the little gadget in the vehicle's official, ludicrously-small tool space but when we needed to raise the car we always applied the quick and efficient Hi-lift. In our more or less post-operated states it was essential to have easy-functioning systems so we held our big jack in great affection. Together with the lengthy handle of the tiny 'authorised' instrument and the spade, it was squeezed inside an old inner tube and chained into a compact pack. The bundle stood on a small ledge, which was welded outside the car, beside Pythagoras's back door. A special clamp higher than the shelf held the whole packet in situ. {You can see this bundle on the back of Pythagoras in pictures: 22 on page 27; and 33 on page 75} and This arrangement was used successfully all round East Africa. But Congo conditions were special: we lost the lot!

We were grundling down a long, narrow, green tunnel of low, overhanging trees:

"What's that rattling sound?"
Stopping immediately we inspected all the chains that secured various bits of equipment round the vehicle and on the roof.
"Everything seems to be intact."
We didn't notice that the Hi-lift's upper clamp had broken so the whole chained-up parcel was now not secured to Pythagoras. It was simply balancing on its step. We drove on.

"This thick foliage overhangs horribly. It seems to be squashing us. I feel as if we're in a carwash with green brushes scrubbing the windows."
"Yes; and the branches trying to get in to poke out our eyes are a so-and-so nuisance."
"I hate having to close the windows. It's stifling in this steamy heat."
We heard a sharp sound.
"Just vegetable detritus snapping beneath the wheels," said Bob and I agreed.

A mere *couple* of miles further on, we routinely reviewed the vehicle as we did whenever we changed drivers:
"OH MOTHER! The shelf supporting the inner tube 'sack' containing Hi-lift, spade, and handle for the small jack has sheared off."
Still chained together within their rubber bag, three absolutely *vital* pieces of equipment were simply no longer with us! It was an unimaginable catastrophe.

"Quick! Go back!"
In the narrow 'gulley' between trees, that was not easy. On each side of the rutted track were high mud banks closely covered with undergrowth and grotesquely intertwined roots; but after a several-point turn we headed round to collect our lost items.
"They're sure to be lying in the middle of one of the deepest and muddiest patches," I said pessimistically.

But although we drove a long way back, reversed and hunted over the region again, then repeated these manoeuvres several times, to the tune of 30 wasted miles, the padlocked bundle had dematerialised! Even if the precious collection had been in a lake we'd have been delighted to see it.

"In this region, that seems totally devoid of humans," said Bob aghast and unbelieving, "the whole caboose has been pinched."
"But... It was an exceptionally heavy package! – Difficult to shift... Surely in so few minutes, and in such an apparently totally unpopulated region, our goods *can't* have been moved!"

Back and forth we went, going further and further on each loop, using up precious petrol and wasting valuable time, becoming more and more distraught, till we realised at last: our *indispensible* items had vanished! There was not any inkling of a path or any break in thick ferns but I was so devastated by the tragedy that, on foot, I started battling into the trees beside the place where we thought the stuff must have dropped.

Frenziedly I pushed aside tangled branches and creepers.
"Don't!" yelled Bob. "There're probably snakes twisted round bushes, and nasty little poisoned Pygmy arrows poised to shoot."
That daunted me, and eventually I returned, dejected and dreadfully worried. I vented my horror by stating the obvious:
"We've lost three essential bits of equipment which could make the difference between life or death. They've just evanesced! "
Deeply depressed we drove on gingerly.

"How many more horrendous Zairian miles to go before we can escape into Central African Republic?"
"Less than 300. Of course if too many detours are forced upon us it'll be more." (We took three and a half more hard and long days battling to the Oubangui River, which was the border with C.A.R.)
"And how far till we reach anywhere that *might* sell a jack – of *any* sort?"
"Just over 600 miles to Bangui, the C.A.R. capital. It depends upon how civilised that is. Perhaps it'll have a shop with some kind of jack."
"One thing's certain: *no* Hi-lift will be available."
"Undoubtedly."
"As well as the Hi-lift, the handle for the little jack was in that bundle that we've lost – so the small jack's unusable. The spade,

which we might need desperately, has gone."
The answer came in grim tones:
"Yes!"
"So now we've no means *at all* of lifting Pythag if we have a puncture or any other trouble: and no way of digging ourselves out of sludge..."
"Yes. We'll be totally stuck if we have complications."
The silence was intense as we guided the Land Rover onwards over horrendous terrain.

****

There were lighter moments.
"Stop a minute, will you?" said Bob. "I have to go behind a bush."
"Help yourself," I replied. "Plenty to choose from."
Bruce was making less than happy noises so he probably needed his nappy changed. From Pythagoras's front shelf my husband seized our ridiculously bright plastic bag containing the toilet roll. I turned to the baby as Bob disappeared behind bracken. An instant later my spouse was back, looking very frightened. A smear of mud on his usually implacable accountant's face emphasised a terrified expression. Dread enveloped me. What had happened?
"Daphne!" he gasped in horrified tones, "I've been stung!"

Oh Heavens! Bob was doomed! I started shivering with shock. My limbs seemed to congeal in terror. Shards of panic spiked in all directions. My thoughts were in disarray:
'The Kisangani anti-snakebite kit ...so inadequate!'
'Can I remember what Dr Hart explained? How to deal with a case of snakebite? – Or scorpion sting? Will I have the sheer guts to cut and scrub and inject? Anyway – unless Bob knows what's stung him how will I know what to put into the syringe? Things will become infinitely worse if I use the wrong serum. He'll die in agony.'
"Where? What got you? Not a snake?"
"I don't know. It nipped me just here..."
He put his hand back to touch his posterior, then *yelled*:
"OW!"

He sounded panic-stricken as he rapidly withdrew his hand. Appalled, trembling and sucking a finger, he exclaimed:
"It's still there! It's *bitten* me again! – *Twice* this time!"

But my own fear had vanished. I was smiling broadly.
"What're you grinning about? It might be something highly poisonous!"
I stretched out my hand and from the seat of his shorts detached a dry twig liberally endowed with vicious thorns like small razor-sharp scimitars. It must have snagged Bob as he passed a shrub. When he put his hand back to show where the 'vile biting aggressor' had attacked him, he pushed the original thorn deeper and another prickle simultaneously 'assaulted' his finger, so he was convinced that some cruel creature had again – twice – injected him venomously.
When I handed him his 'dangerous foe he gulped and did an amazed double take.
"What? – I – er - " he gobbled.

53. Loaded dugout passing in front of a ferry which, having long since lost one propeller blade, was now deep in reeds.

5. African Fish Eagle. (Acrilic.)
A huge, handsome and iconic bird of African waterways.

23. Hammerkop. (20 inches from beak tip to end of tail.)
The basement lodger.

CHAPTER TWENTY THREE

Bonobo ferry. Drunken policeman.

Cotton ginnery. Bats.

Bob again slammed down the knobs to bring into use four-wheel drive *and* reduced gear.
"I think these bits of road round Likati are the most dangerous we've encountered so far," he panted.
"It's the awful teetering bridges high above rocky rivers that petrify me."
"Which are worse: the horrible, heart-stopping bridges or the rickety ferries?"
It was a moot point.

One midday we needed to cross a river where the only sign of life was a common hammerkop poised on a semi-submerged stump. These amusing coppery-brown birds have skulls shaped like elongated hammer tops and this one turned its ridiculous head this way and that as its beady eyes considered whether or not we were friendly. Hammerkops often make untidy nests by burrowing into vast disorganised bundles of twigs, which magnificent African Fish Eagles call home; but that day we saw only the basement lodger. No Fish Eagles were in view. There were no humans either. For some time, as usual, we had been bashing along through a seemingly unpopulated region of all-encroaching vegetation. So how would we get across this river?

"Damn! There's not a soul to get the pontoon moving"
"Did you *expect* anyone to be around?" asked Bob sarcastically.
"No. We haven't yet found barge haulers at hand."
"We must at least be grateful, I suppose, that the craft, such as it is, is on our side of the river."
"Honk the horn. Maybe that'll summon them."

An urchin bursting from nearby reeds gave us a minor fright. He was clutching a stout bamboo pole, and testifying to his skill with that inappropriate rod, he had some small fish strung on a long grass stem.

"Here, sweeties for you," I offered – in Africanised Belgian French. "You find men for pulling ferry?"

Clutching the bribe, he scurried off to locate – we hoped – villagers who might be willing to form a barge crew. Bob hated delays so to avoid 'wasting time' we took the chance to eat lunch.

"D'you think he's an enterprising lad lying in wait beside the crossing place hoping for reward?"

"Very unlikely! But you can be certain that he isn't posted to round up any chaps who'll agree to act as ferrymen. That would be too much like efficiency."

"Make Pythagoras give voice again. It might speed things up a bit."

In countries further south and farther east buses, grossly overloaded with everything from mattresses to livestock on their roofs or suspended precariously at their sides, were wobbling towers like blowsy women nearly overbalancing on stilettos; but in Zaire we were aware of no public transport. It seemed that people travelled only in private dugouts.

While we ate on that slimy river bank a canoe came upriver, carrying two paddlers, three other men, a goat, two bicycles, several sticks of bananas, some chickens tied unkindly by their legs to a shoulder pole, and two sad stakes on both of which were speared several bodies of little smoked bonobos. Of course we didn't know that they could have been Ebola carriers. Each tragic corpse was scarcely bigger than Bruce so the sight and smoky smell of those pathetic dead apes upset me enormously but there was nothing we could do about their fate. The awful vision has haunted us ever since. Alas, the practice of eating smoked monkeys continues.

The dugout was hauled up through mud and everybody vanished into thick vegetation. Where the devil did they go? Among the astonishing load there was a woman carrying the most enormous sack of yams. As usual elsewhere in Africa, women in Zaire were beasts of burden. Here – like Masai,

Kikuyu and Ethiopian ladies – they used straps across their foreheads to help support on their backs unbelievable weights that bent them double. Heads down, eyes permanently fixed on the ground, they plodded forward apparently immured to their lots. With each step their vast loads rotated left and right. What would they have made of any talk about "Women's rights?"

Fifteen minutes after the youth had disappeared we had finished lunch and, wonderful to narrate, soon afterwards the ferry team appeared with *Monsieur le Capitaine* swaggering, staggering and grumbling in the rear.

"*Merci beaucoup*. Here's a piece of paper for you."

The boy was overjoyed to receive such a 'prize' for his efforts. Children always ran after us with begging hands crying out for *"Papier!" "Papier!"* Any scraps would do for schoolwork – even torn bits of old newspaper were received with grateful capers. All over Zaire in 1971 there was a dismal lack of almost everything.

Our relief at having a crew was short-lived. First we had to drive through liquid ooze to reach the pontoon. Two men held it more or less still. The others stood poised to push us if we bogged down. Then we were stunned to realise that *the deck scarcely existed*. Decomposing mats had been thrown over barrels that wobbled independently and gave no secure tyre hold. Sluggish movement showed that some drums were waterlogged. The casks were roped together – yes – but exactly *how* decayed were the links? How long since the knots had been tied? And how imminently were the worn strands about to snap? Every time the men yanked on the fraying hawser to pull us across, the barrels jiggled so Pythagoras teetered and seemed on the point of slithering sideways into the turbid depths.

With one accord Bob and I looked at each other and said: "Bruce!"

What if the vehicle slipped overboard? We'd never get the baby out in time. Crocodiles? Leeches? Vile viruses? Looking at the knotted, thick-stemmed weeds and the gungy water I realised that any idea I might have had of swimming with the baby in my arms was doomed to disaster; but Bruce's plastic foam mattress and the basket would float – for a time anyway.

Happy to stop pulling, the men watched passively. On that short pontoon there was little room to open Pythagoras's rear door and then extract the bulky Fish Basket, but that was achieved – with difficulty, skids and gasps – and nothing rolled out to splash and sink. Then we stood unsteadily on the insecure 'deck' clutching the basket handles and hoping that if the worst came to the worst Bruce would survive – like Moses.

Driving off safely seemed impossible. It was first an act of apparently unjustified hope, and then of unbounded relief!

35. Bondo cathedral –
so much grander and so much better-built than the hovels of the people. Even before battles ripped through the country were there ever enough worshippers to fill it?

Elsewhere the *Bondo District Chief* (note his position) appeared on the riverbank to share our ferry when he heard us hooting to summon a crew. He told us how to reach the nearby Bondo Mission.

"They'll let you camp there," he advised affably as he marched off the raft and turned down a footpath.

We discovered a vast, splendiferous religious compound of many impressive brick buildings where all the White Fathers had been gruesomely massacred. Standing above us on imposing steps an African Monsignor, magnificently, yet incongruously, garbed in puce taffeta, greeted us with exquisite courtesy but said:
"*Je regret infiniment* the *Bondo District Chief* (sic) has forbidden anyone from taking 'tourists'."

Seeing our disappointed faces looking up at him the lordly cleric relented and suggested:
"Try the town's disused cotton ginnery."

We had trouble finding the cotton ginnery compound and were much hindered by a disgustingly drunk policeman with unveiled lecherous desires. Having heard the priest's suggestion, despite his condition, he managed to locate us, and then behaved repulsively as we started to pitch camp. He did his damnedest to creep into Pythagoras beside me when I fed Bruce.
"Get OUT!" I yelled, terrified – for my child and for myself. The baby couldn't possibly have realised what was going on but I suppose that some instinct told him that his sustenance was threatened; and he wasn't having that! As he guzzled greedily one side of his face was shoved hard against my breast but he gazed towards the intruder out of the corner of his one free eye with a look of such malignancy that, had I not been so intent on hiding my fear, I would have had to laugh. Avoiding the boozer's waving hands, I edged further into the vehicle and stretched my leg along the seat with the shoe towards our nauseating, stinking and vociferous visitor.

Bob made threatening motions. But, though rapidly becoming desperate, I remembered the many warnings we had received:
"Whatever happens steer completely clear of the Police."
"They're the worst thugs of all."
"Whatever you do never report anything to the Law Officials. You'll find that it is *you* who are arrested."
So I begged my husband:

"Let him be. Punishment for laying hands on a policeman is probably grim: doubtless incarceration in a frightful jail then disappearance in painful, unmentionable circumstances."
Although very upset, it was better to refrain from clouting the reeking man. Bob still simmered so I added:
"Besides, he's much stronger and bigger than either of us."

Suddenly the terrifying nuisance was silent, staring blankly. Instead of flailing about he was standing like a stone, mouth open and clutching Pythagoras's toolbox. From there his lower body was hidden from me but Bob exclaimed in disgust:
"He's wetting himself!"

The peaceful moment quickly over, distressful shouting staggering about, and attempting to get into the car, resumed. What to do? How to rid ourselves of the abominable fellow? The situation was horrifying. With great self control Bob tried to move the intruder gently. We were at our wits' end.

The sympathetic ginnery watchman reported matters to a superior who, on seeing Bruce, extremely kindly insisted:
"Come with me. I will show you the Ginnery's Rest House."

It was a derelict, unplumbed and completely empty hangar with a mud floor, where bales of cotton had once been stored. Under the circumstances we found it very acceptable. Extracting a heap of food, air mattresses, bedrolls, and night things onto the ground and locking Bruce inside the car, we shouldered off the foul policeman, who, luckily, seemed to have lost the ability to grab anything. Avoiding his staggering attempts to seize us we ferried items into the shed while the watchman guarded what was left of our belongings in the pile. The tottering menace made determined efforts to share the barn, but we dodged the fellow's frightening lurches. As we carried in the final item, Bruce, in his basket, Bob yelled:
"Look out! He's got in!"
"Oh Goodness!"

The cunning guard, who presumably decided that the beast was in no state to remember what had been done to him, finally extracted the hiccupping and burping farter by comically poking out the officer of the law with a long, strong stick.

Maybe it's not only in Britain that we say:
"I wouldn't touch it with a barge pole!"

Clanging shut the metal door, we saw with immense relief that it had a bolt. Subsequent throwing-up noises, prolonged and nauseating, roused no sympathy, but it was necessary to watch our step the next morning. By then the menace himself was not around, but we had heard no yodelling hyenas nor sounds of bones being crunched during the night so presumably someone had dragged him home.

We spent a comfortable night unmolested by any two- or four- legged animals but under siege from battalions of vicious mosquitoes. The echoing, corrugated warehouse was very far from insect-proof.

"I wish we were in the tent with netted door and windows," grumbled Bob.

"That wouldn't keep out the disgusting policeman."

Surrounded by dozens of smouldering mosquito coils we looked as if we were holding a wake or carrying out some black magic ritual. Streaming eyes were a small price to pay for a bite-less night.

There were only a few rents in the roof so when the most almighty thunderstorm struck before dawn we appreciated the dry sections of the hangar; but as we tossed in our sleeping bags we wondered what erosion was doing to the 'roads'.

Below the roof struts at the far end of the shed was a squirming collection of small velvety bodies: thousands of bats, emitting very faint squeaks. They used the roof cracks to sweep out of the barn at sunset and to return en masse just before dawn. The heap of droppings that lay below their perches didn't stink enough to make us choose to risk camping. No doubt after insects that were attracted by light from our paraffin lamp they flittered overhead inside the barn; but they didn't worry us, and we had no idea that they were prime carriers of Ebola. Luckily the creatures didn't drop their bodily fluids because it is contact with such liquids that transmits E.H.F.

The next morning it was our turn to present the slapstick. It was dark inside the barn so we didn't wake till 06.30, then suddenly overcome by diarrhoea, we both had to race to the very unusual luxury of a nearby rubbish pit – much to the amusement of the locals who had no inhibitions about watching and laughing. We could not account for this brief indisposition which, luckily, did not last beyond breakfast time.

When no convenient rubbish pit was at hand scrabbling through dense foliage to reach a decent distance from the tent to answer a call of nature could take time as well as make the imagination run mad, especially after dark. Even if the nightly storms were not obliterating moon and stars, precious little light filtered through the thick canopy. Suddenly all sounds that until a few minutes ago were just 'normal' jungle noises, became fraught with evil significance. You stood (or squatted) quivering as you wondered which part of your anatomy was about to be bitten, stung or otherwise attacked.

29. Python in bamboo.
Note the *small* Giant Snail on bottom right. Some are poisonous

Fortunately it was daytime when I once ventured only just behind a stand of cycads that was growing right beside the track. About to raise my skirt and lower my underwear I noticed a strange sort of root that didn't seem to belong under bamboo. After a double take it turned out to be the swollen stomach of a soundly sleeping python. It had obviously enjoyed a tremendous meal and so wasn't likely to stir for a very long time. Moving circumspectly, I selected a spot from which I could keep a clear watch on its coils and carried on with my performance.

Bob was blowing up air mattresses when, still impressed by the python, I tottered back to camp.

"You brought the skin, I hope," he said, his finger over a valve. "Your mother would like a fine python-skin handbag."

True. But at the moment her thoughts were far from fashion. Having at last rallied after the operation, her husband had now suffered a serious relapse. Would this hospital nightmare never end? Would her daughter and grandson arrive in time? How could she alert them of the desperate situation? She couldn't.

That rubbish pit outside the ginnery's shelter was unique because such amenities were not usually needed anywhere. If we had unwanted containers we kept them until we met humans then gave the cans to villagers or bartered them for local products, though heaven knows, we saw little in the way of crops. An empty fizzy drink bottle could be exchanged for a hand of bananas, a beer bottle for eggs or a piece of yam. Sometimes a small pawpaw was available. Any rubbish in any way edible we placed in a pile and it vanished overnight down the gullets of visiting creatures, probably four-footed.

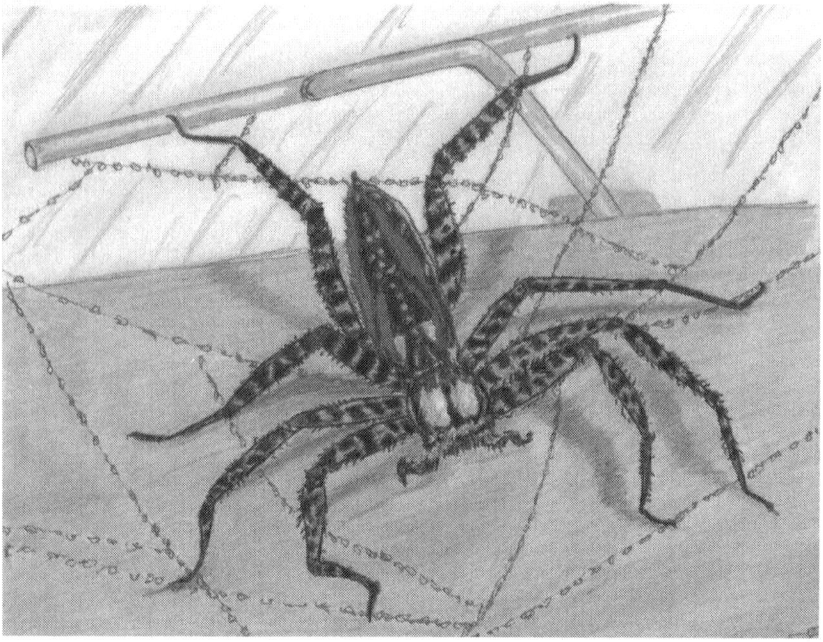

34. Yet another arthropod that might have harboured Ebola! What a good thing we knew nothing of that terrible disease or of how it is transmitted. I have to admit that the small windscreen wiper exaggerates her size – a little! I copied her shape and colours faithfully from a photo.

Thriving everywhere in Zaire were/are so many creatures of so many species which could/can carry Ebola and other nightmare illnesses that it's amazing that anyone remains alive in the Congo!

CHAPTER TWENTY FOUR

Cattle truck tourists. Gas stoves. Cannibals

When we returned from the rubbish pit I noticed a veritable galaxy of diamonds. I'm sorry about the mixed metaphor but that is how it's described in my diary and the words recall very vividly the dewdrops on a spider's wondrous 'palace'. Early light that crept out from below clouds set them sparkling.

"Dear me!" I exclaimed. "Come and look at this *enormous* web."

Beautifully woven, it stretched over Pythag's bonnet, from windscreen wipers, across the spare wheel to the toolbox and extended to the replacement springs on the far side. Its incumbent was also huge. Forgetting that spiders are my least favourite form of evolution I had to admit that the lady in possession was *magnificent*. Apart from a large body she had amazingly long legs that she spread as brazenly as a blonde out to seduce the lifeguard on the beach. Her colour scheme was scarlet, lemon yellow and black – very elegant!

"Well, well, well," said Bob. "We don't want *that* joining us in the Land Rover."

He looked round for a long stick, but in the plethora of trees and welter of undergrowth there was nothing suitable.

"Sod's law!"

Fetching the watchman's 'barge pole' from inside the hangar I offered that to my husband.

"I won't deprive you of the pleasure," he said backing away. Well, *I* wasn't going to admit to being afraid! Gingerly I waved my weapon at the creature. She raised front legs in a threatening gesture. Thank goodness I didn't then know that spiders can carry E.H.F.!

"I hope it's not a jumping kind," said my valiant spouse from a safe distance. An attempt to throw him a disparaging look probably failed because I was scared to take my eyes off our striking visitor.

It was easy to wind some of the web round the pole. Madam Spider shinned up one of her lines and then started

running along the rod – not away from her persecutor but towards me.
"Oh, lummy!" I muttered.
Holding the baton before me, I charged towards bushes like a mediaeval knight with lance poised. Screeching children scrambled for safety. The stick dropped into vegetation and I breathed again when my passenger lowered herself by a thread and scuttled away.
"Phew!" gasped Bob. "Well done!"

Later, as we bounced along, he announced:
"Do you realise – since leaving Buta, 30 hours ago, we haven't met a single other traveller?"
"What's so special about that? We usually go *days* without seeing another vehicle."
"But this stretch is part of the main north-south highway across Africa. Those teachers I chatted with at that ghastly prostitutes' 'hotel' said that very occasionally convoys from Europe, always going south, come through this part of Zaire heading straight into East Africa. They never seem to come back! We'd have emerged onto this road at Buta if we'd been forced to deviate into Uganda to avoid LGT."
"Oh."

The next day we *did* meet trekkers: two enormous lorries full of indescribably filthy young people who had paid for the adventure of a trans-Africa trip. Transported rather like cattle in the backs of laden trucks, they sat on hard benches along the sides, looking inwards, across a central pile of luggage and towards their many fellow trekkers who were facing them. They were keen to talk to new faces.
Bob noticed:
"Your 3-tonners have roofs and sides made only of canvas – precious little protection in the case of an accident or in bad weather."
"Sure! We have to dodge quickly to avoid branches. They whip inside and try to spike out our eyes," said one young man who seemed to think that was a huge joke.
Wonderingly I remarked:

"Those rolled-up sides of heavy canvas sag horribly between the 3 or 4 straps that are supposed to support them. Don't you get frustrated watching so little of the country that you're crossing?"
"You bet! Each of us only sees a small segment of view on the far side of the vehicle."
"I'm O.K.," volunteered one cheery woman. "I've got the seat at the rear so I can look out backwards. – That's if the back flap is up. Anyway – what is there to see in this vertical morass of greenery?"

We couldn't believe our eyes when we studied the conditions under which they were travelling and the apathy with which they accepted their lot! Land Rovers, and even cars with so-called 'sealed' windows' were revolting enough in dusty conditions, but the agony of sitting in those 'flaps only' vehicles when crossing the desert or on gravel roads can only be appreciated by folk who have experienced the all-permeating grit of such conditions. As for wet situations...
"Doesn't the rain soak you?"
"Yeah! Equatorial downpours're pretty emphatic, aren't they?"
"Our canvas walls are useless. The deluge drives straight in."
We goggled anew! No wonder they were so disgustingly dirty! This type of transport was phased out at home ages ago – even before Nyasaland had turned into Malawi.

"Most of you seem to be suffering from inflamed eyes? Is that because of the dust on the roads further north?"
"Yes," confirmed a lanky female unwinding herself from a very cramped corner. "It's absolutely devastating. You can't imagine how awful it is. If we're not skidding about in mud we go along in a huge cloud of beastly filth. It completely stops any view there might be sideways. Of course we can't see forwards because of the cab."
"Would you like some boracic acid crystals?"
"What's that?"
"You dissolve some in warm water and when it's cool enough you bathe your eyes in the solution. It calms inflammation. We always carry an enormous packet and aspirin tablets and quinine pills, in case we come across any ailing natives."

The girl seemed offended.
"We have medics with us," she muttered, and turned away.

Bob studied the brochure that their doctor gave us. "Those people have been carefully selected. They wouldn't have *us*. It states here that over-30s are not accepted because they are unable to bear the hardships – physical or psychological."
I had a ready reply to that:
"Oh well! Bruce would qualify!"

The pamphlets also set out their approximate programme and I saw with real envy that they took about twice as long as we did over each section. How I would have liked to spend time taking photos and to enjoy the scenery and sites! (Bloody Schedule!) Yet when asked about how they passed the time when they weren't bumping along, the travellers were lethargic and couldn't describe anything untoward.
"When we're not stuck in mire or broken down we just grind on and on and on, with scarcely any pauses. We're so *tired*," they moaned. "If we're not being bashed forward we just do our best to get some sleep."

We could have told them a thing or two about being shattered but I found their attitude very odd! Rather than take an interest in their journey they collapsed into zombies or flirted frantically, the many women vying shamelessly for the attention of a handful of men. (Is that distribution of the sexes revealing? e.g. about bravery? curiosity? or being tied to jobs?)

Meeting this passive flock was galling. We believed that our expedition was special, but now we realised that these passengers considered the north-south journey as merely some sort of extended holiday. They hadn't pondered deeply about possible routes where there might be less warmongering or fewer rainstorms, nor spent months writing to distant embassies and waiting for replies.
"Did you have trouble getting your permits and so on?"
"Permits?"
"Entry visas, permission to cross various countries, health documents – things like that."
They laughed scornfully.

"Oh no! The organisers arranged everything. It doesn't take long if you go to the embassies in London."

Tent poles and other long items were lashed to the outsides of their trucks making Bob and me wonder how much experience the leaders really had because that clutter must surely have tangled terribly with foliage as the wagons bashed through Zaire's clinging vegetation. (Trekker companies existed only briefly. A few years later they gave up. After decades others, hopefully better organised, started.)

"I suppose you didn't have to consider what mechanical spares and medicines to carry, or how to pack them, or what adjustments to make to your vehicles?"

They stared at us.

"Of course not!"

One bedraggled young brunette explained:

"I was interviewed, examined medically, paid my money, bought a bedroll, received a clothing list, and turned up in time to clamber aboard lorries supposed to be huge and powerful enough to get through terrible conditions – not that we *have* overcome the millions of rotten spots."

Her male companion added:

"We often have to bust a gut digging and shoving. It's f----g exhausting."

Indeed, we'd heard that those occasional big transports full of once-eager, but now worn out, holidaymakers broke down frequently and then passengers and drivers depended on the kindness of locals to help with repairs, provisions and heaving the vehicles out of quagmires. They were not it seemed, generous with their thanks, verbal or monetary. No wonder they were unwelcome and the prey of thieves.

In Zaire such passers-through had rendered 'tourist' a dirty word so we learnt to tell locals that we were *travellers* going to visit my brother in Nigeria. This was perfectly true. Acceptable to family-orientated Africans, it transformed a potentially hostile encounter into a welcoming reception.

The groups operated in convoy and this lot were waiting for a third lorry to catch them up. They were shocked when they realised that *we* plugged away on our own with no other vehicle at hand to help if things went wrong.

"B---y H--l! Who yanks you out? You'll die when illness hits."

"Presumably between the pair of you, you are experienced drivers, a trained mechanic, and a doctor or nurse," said the organisers snidely. "It must be hard to fit all those qualifications into just one couple."

"Well – er..."

"We wouldn't dream of travelling without those experts."

I had a mad urge to reply:

"We have a baby instead!"

Maybe we were a teeny bit jealous of the lazy life and careless approach of these 'package tourists'. But we very quickly realised that:

"You know – we'd be bored out of our minds if we were among them."

"Yes. Our driver has to be constantly ready to react to all sorts of unexpected dangers and the passenger is always alert to warn about anything unusual. Sometimes I find that it's actually more stressful being the passenger than it is being the driver."

"Oh definitely. But less physically demanding usually."

"Yes."

"I'm not surprised they had 'shell-shocked' expressions," observed Bob after we had left them. "Produced partly by the effects of these trans-continental 'roads', I suppose; but doubtless mainly by the boredom of sitting for hours looking at just a narrow strip of foliage or at dull canvas."

Perhaps we had the same stare-eyed, frizzled-hair appearance; but having to do our own driving, difficult and tiring though it was, never allowed us to become jaded, as those apathetic young people obviously were. We also had to find out routes and possible tourist attractions for ourselves. They just sat and were taken (if the organisers felt like it) – or got stuck!

The trekkers' plans avoided 'the tough bits' of the journey. Three days later Pythagoras crossed the fast, deep and wide Oubangui River at Bangassou *on dugouts.* It was a romantic and exciting 'voyage' but the 'tourists' had used a large motorised ferry at Bangui – very dull! They would avoid LGT by deviating into East Africa, and some of the holidaymakers couldn't wait to reach more civilised roads.

Apart from complaints about the treatment they had received from locals they had horrendous, as well as less awful, tales.

"Getting firewood's b----y difficult," they groused. "In the sodden environment, it's damned hard to find anything that'll burn."

"The forest's so hellish thick! It's challenging actually getting into the effing trees to find dead branches."

"And a forager never knows if his hand is going to land on a snake lurking vilely along some innocent-looking bough."

"I'm terrified of stepping on fire ants, puff adders, scorpions..."

We were grateful because, by gathering whatever material we noticed during the day, we could fairly easily fulfil our needs for a small fire in the evening; and if everything was just too wet, we could always fall back upon our little gas stove. That heater contributed merrily to the many rattles that accompanied our progress. Convenient, disposable containers of Bluet cooking gas had not yet come our way so our miniature steel gas cylinder had to be topped up from time to time.

Usually, between trips, I just went to the local factory where, after huffing and puffing about this not being a normal task, reluctant workers filled it. That was fine in Addis Ababa where I bought the stove, but when I tried to replenish the gas in East Africa, a different valve was needed and to obtain an adaptor took much time and trouble. The same happened in Rhodesia, and South Africa and then in Malawi, till I had a supply of various (brass) adaptors hanging like conkers on a string round the neck of the cylinder. This made for an original necklace; but although it clinked against the metal cylinder with great verve, as a musical instrument it lacked something in tone! We used the stove as sparingly as possible since we could never be sure that our collection of valves would include one to suit the factory of the country in which we might need a refill.

In Bangui (Central African Republic) I was returning dejected from the gas factory wilting in the saturated heat with a large hold-all and a weighty Bruce on one arm and a heavy, unfilled cylinder with its clanking appendage in the other hand, when a cheerful local lady fell garrulously into step beside me. Not wanting to cause an international incident, I broached the subject of cannibalism very circumspectly. Her round, good-natured face splitting into a delightful smile, she happily confirmed that it was practised thereabouts. (In 2014 TV and radio reports of International Media proved it was still common.)

"Yeah-eh. Of course!" chortled my well-built, temporary friend. She passed her tongue over her lips as she mentally appreciated the flavour of a tasty human muscle. "If you're Christian the Moslems eat you. If you're a Moslem the Christians will get you."

Against plump, healthy, chocolate-brown cheeks her teeth were wonderfully white, beautifully straight and LARGE!

I looked up at her feeling like Little Red Riding Hood.

"All the better to eat you with, my dear!"

54. Hoopoe (length 10-12 inches) Eats insects, including larvae of Processional Caterpillars that attack pines.

CHAPTER TWENTY FIVE

Bondo mechanic. Jacks. Drinking problems. Bridges.

Jungle Juju. Official wants me to become his Wife N° 4.

The Hi-lift calamity happened during the day that we reached Bondo, where the mellifluent monsignor had re-directed us to the disused cotton ginnery. We were distraught. It was *essential* to find some way that would enable us to use the small jack if we were reduced to such straits; but Bondo had nothing in the way of a mechanic, not even at the barracks which we approached with great reluctance. So despite the rebuff of the night before, we decided to brave the Mission and see if it had a workshop that could perhaps make some sort of handle for the little official jack.

The fulsomely bearded Zairian brother in charge of Mission Maintenance was an excellent fellow. He soon got his furnace roaring and by 10.30, without electrical power for his lathe, had turned out a far better model than the tricky-to-manage handle we had lost – the one that Land Rover provided with their conventional jack. For this the black genius asked only one Zaire but we insisted on giving him double and had been prepared to pay 5Z. While the good brother worked we toured Bondo village vainly seeking to buy a shovel and beer.

Hunting for booze might seem strange – and failing to find it in this ale-sodden land was even more peculiar – but neither is as odd as the comment in Bob's diary:
"Couldn't get beer. This may result in a drinking problem."

By rearranging our packing we had managed to wedge the holed 25 litre water container on its side with the shattered corner uppermost. Into that tank we carefully poured 6½ litres of filtered water, which the Mission kindly gave us.
"You must boil it," suggested our workshop friend.

When he learnt that we were planning to leave Zaire from further north he also advised:

"The border with C.A.R. is the Oubangui River. The Immigration Office is ten miles *before* that. After the Mongo ferry look for a small sign on the left."
Without his warning we would certainly have missed: "*l'Immigration*" scribbled on a tiny scrap of bark and nailed insecurely, high up on a tree. We'd have had to retrace ten difficult miles from the border. Terrible idea! Under present conditions that could mean a day's journey.

The Congo didn't let us escape easily. Before we reached "*l'Immigration*" Zaire had several stings in its tail. One was a series of ghastly bridges in the final stages of collapse. Their top layer consisted of tree trunks placed parallel to the direction of traffic – which would have been fine if they'd been fixed and if the entire stratum had existed. But no! Between the rotting trunks were gaps because only 3 or 4 logs remained and they were located to suit the width of big lorries that might pass once in a blue moon. Our wheel span was smaller and the chance of slithering off the slippery logs into intervening spaces was great. Far below, a chaos of tumbled boulders rose from deep, often foaming, water. Falling would smash Pythagoras to pieces. We dreaded such disaster.

It was easy to understand why there were only 6 vehicles registered in the region north of the Mongo Ferry and two of those were out of commission.

By fantastic good luck, plus desperate pleas to Heaven, we slipped only once. There was a horrifying slide-and-sinking sensation. I'm sure my heart stopped. Were we about to skate right off the high bridge and crash down onto those phenomenal boulders? Fortunately, before we skidded over the edge, decayed logs crumbled to dust and our rear wheels suddenly fell about a foot. Pythagoras jolted and stopped. The situation was so 'fraught' that there was absolute silence. Shocked, we opened doors gently to maintain equilibrium. Cautiously we stepped out onto slimy wood. Well and truly jammed, several metres above the rock-strewn flood of evil-looking water, the vehicle's springs were balanced on logs with the back wheels dangling between decomposing tree trunks. The situation was desperate.

"The only chance of getting out of this is to hoik Pythagoras up and then drive off the jack. It's a ghastly thought and it will probably ruin the little instrument – the only one we have now."

37. One of the smaller, lower and better bridges. Most spanned boulder-strewn, and sometimes rough water.

"We'd better make some firm stand for the pathetic toy. Why in Hades do the manufacturers supply such a useless 'gimmick'?"
"Well, maybe in this unique situation it's actually small enough to be exactly what's required."
I got a sarcastic grunt in reply.

There might have been giant boulders in that particular river but we needed just ordinary stones. All round was apparently rock-less ooze. I stretched the net over the Fish Basket before we set to work then, for *half an hour* we battled to find solid lumps – a tricky task when one is surrounded by seemingly stone-free squelchy jungle. Maybe there were plenty of chunks invisibly buried beneath plants and sunk in mud.

38. Jungle Juju.

When the Hi-lift etc was taken we had discovered that, no matter how deserted it may seem the jungle is *never* without people. This fact was drummed in on another occasion when we'd been bumping along for many miles with the feeling that there was nothing other than monkeys, birds, butterflies and animal scats anywhere in the whole of the vast surrounding forest. Suddenly, before us was an isolated clearing, utterly devoid of trees or huts. The unusual utter bareness was in itself a shock. But worse! There on beaten mud, standing alone and mysterious, was an eerie 'juju'. Helmet-shaped objects, each tufted with yellow 'hair', were impaled high on the tops of long, sinuous poles that rose from a ground-level 'cage' of bent sticks.

"The severed head is a potent magical symbol... (It) generates strong psychological reactions..." (From Howard Reid's fascinating: *The Dragon King.)*

What we saw were only *stylised* skulls but the effect upon us was just as great as the fear that curdled the blood of ancient Celts, Elizabethans and others when they saw a genuine spiked head. Inherited ancestral sensations from our most antiquated pasts conveyed such forcible impressions of weird ceremonies that shivers seized our spines. It was further proof that somewhere out there not too far away, were people with blood-curdling customs. We drove hastily past, relieved not to have arrived when witchcraft rituals were being performed.

Not only in the depths of the jungle but anywhere in the African bush you may imagine that you are hundreds of miles from any other human. You step out of the car to go behind a boulder, and before you have finished your pee, you are being observed by at least one pair of inquisitive eyes.

To our amazement, as we laboured to create a stable platform on the bridge below Pythagoras, we now consciously *enjoyed* a similar experience. Gradually, through the drizzle, several Zairians congregated to stare. When we were satisfied that the support would hold, and, using the 'toy', had jacked up the vehicle, for a fee of 1Z and 20 cigarettes, they were delighted to push like mad. I suppose they didn't imagine what might happen if the vehicle slewed sideways. Fortunately this didn't occur, and, with enormous care and effort we jerked off the jack onto logs and slithered off the bridge. I nursed the engine while Bob recovered an only slightly squiffy jack. Fervently we prayed that we would not need to try to use that lifting device in any way ever again. We had no other; but ominously the map showed many more rivers ahead.

According to Michelin, we were now supposed to be emerging from the jungle and – what delighted us even more – out of the Rains as well. Although an endurance test, the Equatorial Forest had been wonderful and fascinating with huge trees, bamboos, creepers, ferns, and flowers. We'd been stimulated by Pygmies, colourful parrots, humming birds, ants and other amazing insects, leaping monkeys, butterflies, arthropods (!) and much more ... But we'd rejoice to leave the turgid air, downpours and mire.

However, Michelin was over-optimistic. The only difference that we noticed was the reduction in the number of butterflies that hitherto had fluttered in enormous swarms at surprisingly high altitudes. They also congregated densely round puddles. The delicate yellow visions loved to sit on animal droppings, hiding their stinking thrones with hundreds of gorgeous, gently-waving wings.

Although Lepidoptera populations decreased, the fearsome bridges and ferries remained as frightful as ever and the Mongo crossing, mentioned by the bearded Vulcan at Bondo Mission, could only be described as 'an experience'!

"The pontoon's planks are completely rotted! And it's yards from the bank!" Bob exclaimed in horror. "We'll have to drive into the river before mounting the slimy deck."

Despite enormous efforts of several men yanking on ropes to prevent motion, the raft sidled off as Pythagoras thrust forward. The craft continued to swing away from land and for a moment our trusty vehicle continued to chase it. Luckily relative movement between raft and car stopped before it was time to swim. When a purchase had (miraculously) been made upon the extraordinary collection of barrels and logs, the various timbers, which were all at sixes and sevens, poked up independently into the air and splayed about as we drove onto them.

"I'll get out and hold Bruce in my arms," I said suiting actions to words. "If anything 'happens' I may be able to save him more easily than if we went down with the car."
"Crocs..." wavered Bob, but his voice petered out.
'Yes,' I thought. 'And Bilharzias and Dysentery and water snakes...'

Weeks later, in Kano (Nigeria), we met a pleasant and enterprising bunch of young Asians who had turned a long-wheel-based Land Rover into a strange six-wheeler by inserting an extra central section. This friendly group, who we met again in the Sahara, started from East Africa, avoided LGT, and were heading for Britain.

The Mongo crossing was such as to ingrain itself upon travellers' minds so with their unusual vehicle it was not amazing that they had suffered particular difficulties there.
"I was driving," Raheen told us bitterly. "We had to get through about a metre of deeper and deeper mush to reach the ferry. As our car began to rise up onto the deck, the pontoon moved away – (We nodded with feeling!) – and broke the ropes, which men were pulling to control movement. Our Land Rover buried its nose in the subsiding, mouldy wood of the barge, which kept on floating away, till our rear sank so deeply into ooze that we came to rest."
He stopped, overcome by his memories.
"I was thinking we would certainly all be drowning," said Mashkal. "Our car was settling down, you know, like a buffalo to be enjoying an extended wallow."
"However did you manage to get out?" we asked breathlessly as we visualised the awful situation. But they wouldn't be drawn on those horrors. Mashkal just said:
"With all of us – five, you know – and the ferrymen assisting, you know, it was taking three hours be extricating the vehicle.

We became very filthy. It was a nightmare! We were waiting several hours for the engine to become dry and then we were working on the car for a terrible long time before it was returning to life."

This particular *Monsieur le Capitaine* was sufficiently sober to try some tricks. He demanded extra money – which he didn't get. Because of his audacity Bob gave him exactly the correct fare of half a crown, and no tip. Had he known, all he had to do to extract more cash was to urge his men in midstream to stop pulling on the hawser.

"I can't believe we've managed across without incident," I breathed at the far side. But I was unduly hopeful. There were some dicey moments as a lot of manoeuvring and punting with bamboo poles ensued before we could disembark – again by splashing through noxious bog.

"That took us over forty minutes just to cross about 200 yards of river," groused Bob.

"Never mind! We had time to admire the hippos and glowering Squacco Heron that was hunched nearby. And we didn't sink!"

55. Dentist's eye view?

For some miles beyond Mongo, thick forest stubbornly continued to clamp round us, and the swamps remained. We were poled (as opposed to the more usual 'pulled') across another expanse of brown fluid that looked more like a delta than a river. It frothed against a beautiful island with sandy edges: surely an ideal spot for crocs; and it swirled round numerous haphazardly scattered, reedy islets whose palms would have struck us as romantic- if we hadn't had eyes only for the end of the 'voyage'.

39 Goliath Heron. (can grow up to two metres.)

A monitor lizard, looking menacing and like a minor dragon, slid suspicously and silently into the depths. Plovers scrutinising the mud and a magnificent goliath heron, standing russet and tall, seemed happy enough but I had definite worries as to whether the crew actually had any more ideas than the plummeting pied kingfisher about where they were trying to take us.

Although looking out carefully, we nearly missed the scrap of bark precariously nailed to a tree that was growing several metres away from the track. Very faded scrawl indicated an inconspicuous *foot*path to *l'Immigration;* so scrunching over tufts of tough grass, we followed the narrow line of mud, and found a hut in a clearing. Glimpsed between palm fronds a welcome patch of usually unseen sky appeared. The trees had, at last, started to thin.

The lonely passport-stamper was red-eyed and not in top form.

"Oh no! Not another drug-dead moron," groaned Bob sotto voce.

Unfortunately, after several over-effusive "*Bon jours*" and many energetic handshakes, even in his befuddled state he discovered a problem, which must have happened in the *mêlée* of the final entry post into Zaire some ten days previously.

"Your passport has not been endorsed," he accused me. "You have never entered Zaire."

"But – you can *see* that I'm here!"

"No. You are not in Zaire!"

Officially I was still stuck in swampy No-Man's Land between Rwanda and Bukavu. Adamantly the man declared:

"You are not in Zaire. I cannot provide an exit permit. You are not allowed to leave the country."

Matters became extremely tricky and the discussion very prolonged.

"You must return to the place where you entered Zaire to have your passport corrected."

That border seemed like a lifetime away.

We explained:

"We do not have twenty days to spare. Also our vehicle will never survive another crossing of Zaire, let alone *two* more squelching, bumping traverses."

Paralysing horror began to seep through us as we realised that we were battling against total impasse. Would we be stranded in this benighted patch of jungle forever? Then Bob had a brilliant idea – but it backfired – horribly!

"You can pretend not to see my wife. She can leave the country with her passport unstamped."

Turning to me he explained:

"You would just have passed through this place – what's it called? – er – Mongo District – and Zaire – like an unseen ghost."

Bob should never have mentioned the word 'wife'. It gave the administrator his counter inspiration:

"She cannot leave. She *must* remain here," he leered. "I need another female."

Chortling and smirking he added gleefully: "Wife Number Four! Baby stays also. Male child. Good for war."

Revulsion! Fear! Our previous alarm tripled. After a stunned moment of dropped jaws we plunged into yet more frantic palaver.

The situation had degenerated from awful to catastrophic when Bob muttered:

"Fetch the whisky."

Deciding to part from his tipple indicated desperation, but was a major inspiration. Liquor was vastly preferable to another woman.

The bleary-eyed bureaucrat grabbed the booze. I seized our documents, and Bob made a dash for the driving seat. Before the fellow realised what was happening, we scuttled out of that hut praying that the nowadays-temperamental Pythagoras would start first go. He did; so in record time we scooted out of the Immigration enclosure, rattled along the footpath, and headed for the Customs Post at Ndu, which was not far from the banks of the Oubangui River.

On the morrow I left Zaire as a wraith – as Bob had suggested. According to documents I never experienced those extraordinary nine and two halves days in the Congo.

45. As we left the jungle the track became unrecognizably good.

CHAPTER TWENTY SIX

Drum beats and weaverbirds.

At last escaping from forest to more open bush country was like emerging from an immensely long tunnel into floodlit Heaven – into our sort of terrain. What bliss! After our flight from the wife-hungry official only a few odd patches of huge creeper-hung rainforest remained before we reached the *Douane* (Customs). It was closed for the night; but this did not worry us as it was too late to attempt the Oubangui crossing.

We camped below large trees that, to our eyes, now accustomed to tightly packed jungle, seemed marvellously spaced. Hadeda Ibis were guffawing from the banks of a stream that presumably ran into the River Oubangui. We would have to cross that the next day. Jacana, (Lily Trotters) their coppery backs aglow in the sunset, with their extra-long toes well spread, were scurrying about on huge floating leaves as if late for appointments. They looked like overwhelmed clerks with hands under coat tails behind bent backs.

"We haven't been able to clean up since the water container disaster and yet another major 'washing machine' spillage." I announced. "I'm going to take advantage of 'running water' to mop Pythagoras."

Bob looked dubiously at the stream's swirling brown supply.

"You'd better lace it liberally with Dettol," he said. Then, pointing upwards, he went on:

"Oh damn it! Pre-dawn alarms!"

Along the bank, reeds and trees were decorated with hundreds of incredibly well-woven grass baubles. This multitude of Weaver Birds' nests dangled and bounced from the very ends of branches. Their shapes are so much like human male genitalia that whenever I hold one up to illustrate my talks the audience invariably sniggers. Each entrance is the tip of the 'penis' and the 'testicles' accommodate the birds. Perhaps the Almighty ran out of designs but it's more probable that the birds evolved the model to thwart hunting predators. A snake seeking eggs or chicks has difficulty reaching its quarry, not only because the thin tips of branches may break under its weight, but also because it's tricky to wriggle *down* in order to find the entrance, and then to wind upwards inside the 'penis' into the 'testicles' where eggs or babies might be hidden.

40. Nests of two different types of Weaver Bird.

The hungry reptile slithering through the Weavers' colony rouses golden pandemonium. Many hundreds of panicking birds scream and fly about frantically, repeatedly dashing down to attack. However, there is a strong chance that the snake will go hungry. Each choosy female scrutinises her wooing male's efforts as minutely as any young couple examines the estate agent's offers. She usually refuses to occupy four out of every five of his beautiful works of art, so lots of nests remain empty and the hunter flickers his forked tongue into many 'desirable residences' in vain. The birds would produce a deafeningly vibrant sunrise but now, after a tremendous 'sleep well' racket, they settled for the night with muted chirps.

"Do you realise," I asked, "how delightful it is to actually *see* the sunset? It's been hidden from us for so long behind the thickest rain forest of Africa, the biggest in the world after the Amazon."

"Yes," Bob replied, "and there's going to be a starry sky later with none of the usual thunderclouds pressing down!"

"Can you hear the faint thumping of a generator?" he asked, "I think it's coming from far across the river?"

"Yes. But I can't see any glimmer of light from over in that direction. Are you sure that Central African Republic really *is* there – just over the water?"

"According to the map, it is."

Was our "longed-for land" really not far away or did we have to plough further through Zaire? As I gazed towards the sound of the throbbing machine, inside me bubbling excitement seemed to match its pulse. If we could get over there we'd have escaped from Zairian horrors. Of course, for all we knew, the problems to be faced in C.A.R. might turn out to be just as bad – or worse! Confused emotions surged: Hope that the Immigration man seeking Wife Number Four wouldn't pursue us; Worry about how we were going to get over the huge river that lay in out path; Concern about what the countries ahead would throw at us; Anticipation of interesting and pleasurable adventures... Who knew what was to come! For the moment – ever unreasoning optimists, we were quietly hopeful.

Over supper, we revelled in familiar sounds of the bush (as opposed to the jungle) and discussed our chances of being able to extend our two-day visas for *Republique Centrafricaine*. That was all that we had been allowed but it would obviously be impossible to cross the large country in so short a time. We'd have worried had we known of the scene that would be play out the next day in the C.A.R. official's riverside hut. However, for the moment, frogs were croaking happily: there were drums beating in the distance, and nearby splashing hippos were apparently enjoying some gargantuan joke. We felt happy and at home.

41. Weaver at work

CHAPTER TWENTY SEVEN

Making the raft.

Nearly out of the jungle we may have been but its soupy atmosphere was still all round. Although there had been only slight drizzle during the night, when we woke on the day that we hoped would see our 'liberation' from Zaire the tent was absolutely soaked both inside and out.
"There's been so much condensation that our sleeping bags are sopping."
"Good thing we had a cover over Bruce's basket."
"Oh well! Don't let's worry about the sodden stuff now. Let's concentrate on crossing into C.A.R."
"Pack quickly. The Customs Office here opens at 7.30. And we don't want to risk yesterday's Immigration fellow turning up."
"Gosh NO! Don't bother to put the tent into its bag. We'll do that later, after we've had a chance to spread it out to dry."

Unfortunately the Customs Official didn't arrive till 08.30 so we wasted an hour of good drying time, and spent it looking anxiously down the road in case the passport man appeared. Luckily, however, the whisky probably rendered him paralytic, and ten miles are a formidable distance when you're in that state.

Dreading more complications, such as the problems we'd faced the evening before, we were mightily relieved and happy to find that although the *Douanier* wasn't a good timekeeper, he was friendly and sensible, and not after another wife! He was also delighted to receive the letters we had brought him from Kisangani.
"I've never had to deal with a vehicle going north," he mumbled, shuffling papers about. "I've only done southbound transports – *entering* Zaire." Then, making up his mind: "Here – *You* fill in the stupid *carnet* for the car."
He was very interested in the camera permits as he apparently hadn't seen such documents before. Having had them explained he ended by ordering:
"Do what is necessary for them."

When that feat had been accomplished – Consternation! Pythagoras had reached the end of his tether and wouldn't start. The Official's underling was delighted to demonstrate rippling muscles and turn the crank handle. Then he kindly suggested:
"Shall I show you the way to the crossing place?"
"No, thank you. It's just a bit further along the track, isn't it? "
"That's right."
"You know that the Oubangui River is deep and fast- flowing without a pontoon?" checked the *Douanier* as, with metallic crashes of unpadded doors, we prepared to drive off.
"Yes. And we've heard that we might have to cross on a raft – possibly contrived from dugouts. Surely that can't be true!"
"But, of course. That is correct."
I think we both probably went a bit pale.

'Forewarned' is not always synonymous with 'prepared' and it came as a shock to reach that un-spanned expanse so wide that the usual type of pontoon dragged over by hauling little by little on a rope could not possibly be used, and so deep that poling across was out of the question.

"Gosh!" I gasped. "Look at all those brownish-green swirls! It's heaps broader than any of the rivers or swamps that we've crossed so far."
"Yes," agreed my depressed husband. "Look!"
He pointed to thick Papyrus plants. Poking above their feathery plumes a weed-festooned funnel and tops of two similarly decorated paddlewheels revealed the whereabouts of a sunken, long-defunct ferry: a depressing sight of despaired neglect. Later we learnt that the boat's only problem was one broken propeller blade.

"There's evidently a powerful current."
"The water looks dreadfully sinister."
"I can't even pretend to be exactly happy at the thought of balancing Pythagoras on a raft made of several wobbly hollowed-out tree trunks; and anyway – where are they?"
"There're two drawn up on the bank over there."
"You must be joking! That's not enough to float us across!"

We fell silent watching another dugout, full of passengers, struggle past near us on the Zaire side.

"See how hard its paddlers are labouring! And it's well out of the main current, so what must it be like in the middle?"

"I hate to think."

As there was no chitchat exchanged across the water between the hard-working travellers and idlers on our bank the primitive craft passed in silence, apart from slight splashes, and occasional echo-y 'clonks' when paddles struck its sides.

Women bashing clothes against rocks in the brown eddies, bottoms pointing skywards, mocked our blank faces and pointed with their heads and wet elbows towards a group of semi-naked men who were lounging in the shade of bushes and tall trees scattered round an open area of dried murram. When questioned, the loafers gestured lazily way down the thickly vegetated northern shore to distant huts clustering amid banana clumps and tall, languid tufts of palms.

"There – maybe – you may find men with dugouts."

How could we contact those potential helpers, so far downstream and on the other side of the river? Another loiterer, when pressed, agreed that, for a fee, he might take us across in his canoe to palaver with the folk on the northern bank. So far so good – if you could describe being paddled across a surging flood in a waterlogged and wobbly dugout as 'good'. But another awkward matter faced us. Somebody had to stay to protect Pythagoras and our luggage. Bob couldn't swim; so logically he should remain on land – with the vehicle. However, as the baby's food supply, I couldn't be separated from the Brat. We were not tempted to take the risk of Bruce disappearing down a crocodile's gaping gullet so there was only one solution: Bob, with grim expression and gritted teeth, very bravely clambered precariously into a small hollowed tree trunk and sat transfixed with unwanted thoughts about toothy reptilian jaws and drowning.

I said someone had to stay to 'protect' our goods. In fact had an attack been made there would have been nothing that either of us could have done to stop it. The guard was just a hopeful deterrent. Pretending indifference but with crossed fingers, I stayed on the south bank with Bruce and Pythagoras, trembling in case wife-seeking officials or locals with similar ideas were about to pounce. The dugout gradually diminished as it was quickly swept far downstream. Although the paddler exerted tremendous muscle power directly towards the further bank movement across the current was painfully slow. Eventually, once Bob was among people whom we had reliably been told were cannibals, negotiations started.

After a while I was devastated to see the canoeist returning *alone*! He nodded laconically and vanished among the trees. Sirens screamed in my head! What had happened to Bob? Bokassa, the ruler of 'that country over there' – currently Dictator and later, from 1976 to 1979 notorious self-styled Emperor – was sometimes said to demand: "Get me a slice of the last Prime Minister's thigh from the deep freeze. That'll cheer me up!"

(Freely interpreted anecdote abbreviated from John Simpson's entertaining book: "*A Mad World My Masters*")

42. Making the raft – or should we call it a 'quinquemaran'?

As Bob hadn't returned, was he even now being chopped and boiled for a village feast? A grisly, gruesome, ghastly idea!

Becoming steadily more and more jittery, I gazed at the distant clutch of thatched roofs. At last a flotilla of large dugouts approached. Terrifying thoughts whipped through my mind:

'Bob was mighty thin. Were they coming to collect Bruce and me to flesh out the contents of the pot?'

With enormous relief I made out that my husband was in the fleet, intact, yet more than happy to disembark.
"I had to bargain hard with a disreputable old villain," he said. "But finally he agreed to accept the equivalent of £9 in Zaires and he offered a good rate of exchange so I shook his filthy, cracked paw and a deal was struck. Probably I paid about ten times the regulation fee – but since we're virtually stranded..."
His hunched his shoulders and held out hands to indicate hopelessness :
"... there wasn't much that I could do."

Under the impression that he was supervising, Bob watched as, without hurry – almost nonchalantly – but with much discussion, the C.A.R. men lashed five of the big dugouts side by side. Then they tied two strips of wood at right angles across the canoes. All was achieved in what seemed a very haphazard, optimistic manner and my poor, incredulous spouse would have been better advised to concentrate on other matters because all he gained was a horrid conviction that the knots would part, the dugouts separate and Pythagoras sink for ever.

Meanwhile, with the help of two locals, I slowly achieved the Herculean task of emptying all our staggering muddle of weighty luggage onto a patch of coarse grass.

When the terrible raft was complete, with his own face set in a stiff-upper-lip rictus, Bob ordered me:
"Don't look so worried."
He drove gingerly down the muddy bank towards two independently rising and falling planks that connected the shore with the boards across the dugouts. Who was most frightened: Pythagoras, Bob or me? Certainly I was absolutely horrified.

43. Emptying Pythagoras

The driver's lips were moving as he aimed down the slime attempting to match the vehicle's wheels with those two sloping timbers that linked squidgy land to the raft. They were narrow. There was no margin for error. Two men walked backwards into the water, watching Pythagoras's approaching wheels and adjusted the spacing.
Probably Bob was muttering:
"Carefully does it... Watch out! Don't skid..."

A bit of courage and a revved engine got him across the planks and aboard the wobbling contraption – but he needed swift reactions.
I watched from the bank, hands to mouth.
"Stop your momentum quickly or you'll drive off the other side into deep water," I whispered urgently.

Rather than be tipped into the flood together with the vehicle Bob cautiously stepped down from Pythag's high driving seat. Remembering that he was not expert at balancing, I was trembling as he stood insecurely on an exposed sliver of one of the timbers that supported the now empty car.
"Don't let that wildly oscillating vehicle push him into the murky flood," I prayed.

Many men up to their waists in water attempted to keep things more or less stable, but canoes dipped ominously and joggled disconcertingly, not simultaneously but each dugout according to its own ideas.
"Aren't you afraid of crocs?" I asked the men.
"Non!" came the reply from a fellow who was pulling a leech off his thigh. "Our splashing frightens them."
Pushed out from the bank, Pythagoras and his driver set off on a heart-in-mouth crossing. My husband smiled as he waved and bobbed off. What was he thinking? Did he wonder if he'd ever see wife and son again?

Teetering on the boards, the Land Rover was facing at right angles *across* the parallel canoes, that is – sideways-on to their line of progress. On the left side of the car Bob, holding on 'by the skin of his toenails' and standing unsteadily on a narrow strip of wood, was near the back of the lashed dugouts. Ten paddlers called responses and worked vigorously in time with the headman's recurring mantra. When they dipped and pulled, the transport, apparently straight out of a Boys' Own Comic or a Tintin book, jerked ahead and, not being tied to the canoes, Pythag swung sideways on his springs towards the 'stern' of the raft. If he'd been sentient he'd have been scared stiff! – Or he *would* have been stiff had he not then inevitably swayed over the other way – towards the front of the improvised ferry. Each time he sashayed left he gave his owner a hefty shove and there wasn't an inch for Bob to stagger.

"Were you worried?" I asked my husband later.

"Petrified!" he admitted. "Every time the Land Rover tilted, I prayed that his springs wouldn't prove soft enough to make the entire contraption topple."

"What about when his swaying made him bash into you – over and over again?"

"It was terrible! I *had* to grab him or I'd have been IN! "

"I noticed, and was scared silly in case even your slight weight might prove to be the last straw."

Thus, progressing sideways, alternately jerking to left and right – or, with respect to the dugouts, backwards and forwards – Pythagoras was gradually taken towards the far bank; and on each oscillation Bob was nearly knocked off the raft into the terrifying water. Several times he muttered:

"Oh, my God! Oh, my God!" If he fell he would immediately be swept dangerously underneath the canoes and provide the crocs with a tiny mouthful.

CHAPTER TWENTY EIGHT

The Oubangui Crossed

So there went Bob – the only one of our expedition who counted in male-orientated Zaire; and there went Pythagoras – our only means of reaching Europe. What was Bob thinking? Did he actually believe that he'd make it to the other side?

For a moment, feeling abandoned, I was just a dot beside the reedy, rushing, rumbustious Ouban... No – it needed a Kipling to describe the situation. I watched the precarious progress of the raft, heart in mouth.

"Ah well," I pulled myself together. "The sooner Bruce and I risk the dugouts the sooner we'll reach – *may* reach – the far bank."

The mammoth mound of our goods was, bit by bit, carried into two very long excavated tree trunks. Nervously I checked that every bundle was well wedged and not likely to tumble off its site. A canoeist and I carefully carried Bruce's basket and jammed it firmly between more bundles in the primitive craft that would take us across. Knowing from experience the very alarming tendency of hollowed-out trunks to roll at the slightest provocation, I hoped desperately that the baby wouldn't move till the 'voyage' was over.

Our cockleshell lurched as I scrambled aboard. For the entire journey it rolled and jiggled, so I sat frozen.

'If Bruce wakes I won't be able to pick him up without upsetting the canoe, and if I let him yell he'll thrash about,' I panicked. To my enormous relief the Brat slept peacefully under (a tree and his net) throughout the whole lengthy process of making the raft and emptying the vehicle. He obligingly stayed asleep while we loaded the canoes, crossed the flood and disembarked up a very steep and slippery mud bank. Thank God it wasn't raining!

The scary 400 m crossing was sheer *Sanders of the River* stuff – or, if you prefer: romantic Africa at its best. It was thrilling! First the powerfully built men paddled like mad, heading against the flow in the lee of the Congolese riverbank.

It made me feel tired to watch their efforts. Then, when we were far upstream, they abandoned the reeds and ventured into the grip of the current. That was a moment to gasp! Our entire chanting flotilla aimed straight across the surging water. Shining black backs were bent, working hard to cross. I found myself panting in time with my crew. If only our parents and siblings could see this!

The current dashed our fleet of 5+1+1 canoes rapidly downstream and separated the raft from the two individual dugouts. The headman's chanting grew fainter. That was alarming but, with our paddlers working tremendously, we slowly made laborious headway across the current. The C.A.R. riverbank seemed terribly far away, the water far too close, and the 25-minute crossing endless and miraculous.

On the far side an unprepossessing mud slope waited. In the nick of time the boatmen skilfully halted our headlong rush downstream, and after a jerk, steered our 'tree-trunk' more directly towards land. In the shallows they battled upstream guiding the bow till it squished softly into ooze. We stopped momentarily and let the current push the stern of our dugout till the canoe was parallel to the bank.

Perhaps on the crossing Pythagoras had been so violently pitched from side to side that he suffered from seasickness. Be that as it may, he was feeling faint and refused to start. Cursing because he didn't have the strength to crank the engine, Bob showed a barely-clad stalwart, whose muscles glistened like wet pitch, how to achieve that dangerous task.

"Have you explained about possible sudden very strong kickbacks from the handle?"

"Don't be daft! How do you expect me to explain anything without knowing his lingo? We'll just have to hope for good luck."

We watched, scared silly in case the powerful engine wrenched unexpectedly and broke the man's hand. What retribution would the tribesmen take if we caused such a ghastly accident?

46. When my dugout was 3/4 of the way across the Oubangui River I risked enough movement to snap Pythagoras approaching the far side. Note the typical pointed paddle, – a style that is used on many Rift Valley lakes, and many African water ways.

47. Pythagoras arrives in Central African Republic.

There was no space for the cranker and no deck for him to stand on. To face Pythagoras's radiator he had to balance, leaning backwards, on one narrow rim of a dugout. (An impossible feat – I would have thought). Shaking planks poised on highly unstable canoes quivered as again and again the fellow yanked at the awkward handle. The paddlers did their best to keep the 'raft' steady. Everybody else froze with bated breath. Finally – Phew! When the motor eventually responded, intense relief overwhelmed us all: participant and spectators alike. There was a sound like a huge balloon being let down as everyone sighed with released tension. Then, in both reduced gear and four-wheel drive, Pythagoras coughed and crawled up the bank. Many singing helpers slithered and pushed as he groaned and growled up the treacherous incline.

A magnificent African Fish Eagle perched royally in a nearby baobab threw his white head back so exuberantly that it bumped his rich russet back feathers. Apparently laughing heartily – the way those birds do – he probably thought:
'Surrounded by all those swarthy legs, all wet, gleaming, slipping and uncoordinated, the vehicle looks like a small lump of haggis being valiantly moved by an army of huge, disorganised, black Driver Ants.'
I suppose grey Pythagoras may have *looked* like a haggis. Bob

and I *felt* more as if the stuffing had been squashed out of us. Crossing Zaire had been an incredible experience. We would not have missed it. But – BOY! Were we glad it was behind us.

"No! Don't get out of Pythagoras," I shouted. "I'll see to the luggage. You keep the engine running."

With much splashing, but luckily with nothing dropped into the slime, the two independent dugouts were unloaded and all our incredible amount of luggage thrown any-old-how into the Land Rover. We distributed sweets and cigarettes as tips, then rejoicing, we bumped up a short road of red mud and rocks.

"Are you feeling a bit shaky after that hair-raising voyage?" asked Bob.

"Not now. Wasn't it exciting? I'm just very relieved. Are you?"

"Shaky – no. Relieved – yes. I'm delighted to have crossed the river, and also because we're shot of Zaire, and because we've now covered roughly two thirds of the way to Scotland."

"Yippee! We're in Bangassou!"

We tottered into the 'new' country with not the slightest idea of what was to come. Central African Republic, Cameroons, and Nigeria still had to be negotiated, before we tackled the terrifying Sahara, which was getting ever closer. That was scaring but at the moment all we could realise was:

"Humid, hot, horrifying Zaire's at last behind us! Surely, nothing ahead can possibly be worse – can it? "

"We'll find out," replied my staid husband. "Which d'you dislike more – desert drought or jungle quagmire?"

A new set of adventures had begun.

It was November 9th. At midnight Bruce would be two days short of 9 weeks old, and we had been on the move for 19 strenuous days. Today we had progressed less than 1 mile from camp site to 'hotel': just one more day in the life of an itinerant brat towards grandparents who might or might not still be alive.

****

If we had known about Ebola Hemorrhagic Fever we'd have been desperately worried when, thirteen days after leaving Ebola territory, we all developed symptoms exactly like those displayed at the onset of that frightful illness, whose incubation period is usually between six and sixteen days. Luckily we knew nothing about nasty viruses so our sanity, such as remained at that stage of our journey, was preserved! In fact we were suffering merely from dreadful colds. That was the only time that any of us were unwell on the whole of *The Daftest Journey*.

****

Note: Since 1971 things have changed enormously in the Congo. People are now as cheerful, outgoing, noisy, and fun-loving as in any other country.

In 2015, however, the Congo's GDP is still the lowest in the world and most people live on less than US$1.00 a day.

48. Bruce *in* his Fish Basket aged 5 months – after we got home. (February 1972)

When the photo was snapped the basket had become a 'boat' and a play area. The padding had been taken out but we obviously hadn't yet got round to removing all the mesh of plasticised washing line, which we had tied round the cradle to strengthen it. What's left of the network shows some of the loops it provided for attaching the rubber straps that went across the top of the basket. They caught falling objects and thus stopped "stuff" from landing on the baby. They also prevented him from bouncing out of the crib when we hit big bumps or fell into huge holes.

49. Little girl in Bangassou, on the bank of the Oubangui River – the first village that we reached in C.A.R.

ACKNOWLEDGEMENTS

This book could never have been written without Bob's diary. It's a meticulous and detailed record, mainly of facts: mileages, times, fuel bought and consumed, state of roads, prices, demographic comments ... and so on.

(My own report tended to be more frivolous. Domesticity didn't allow me time at day's end to write much in my official, foolscap, hardback record book, so my notes consisted mostly of observations and sketches scribbled as we went along, often on the back of Bob's marvellous Rhodesian King Size cigarette boxes. My comments, nearly illegible because of the Land Rover's lurches, described people, flora, fauna, events and trivial incidents.)

Jim Wallace and Bruce himself have helped wonderfully and boosted morale whenever I felt like throwing the computer into the sea. I offer them both my heartiest thanks.

The Guardian Angels just happened to be Yorkshire types because I have a friend who can write the Yorkshire twang. No offence is intended to anyone from that fine county (which produced both my much-loved sisters-in-law) and I am heartily grateful to Kathryn Stych for her translation of my lines into dialect.

My abetter and very useful critic, Birgitta Strausser was fabulous at encouraging me. Thank you, Birgitta. You kept me going.

To Bruce, the hero of this tale, again heartfelt thanks – for surviving the ordeal through which we dragged him!

And of course – Pythagoras: strong and sturdy – carrying on regardless of atrocious terrain – he enabled the entire adventure.

Long live Land Rovers and mad adventurers!

****

50. Diagram to show the random way in which Ebola viruses intertwine with each other and wind round themselves.

APPENDIX

Bald and Bloody Facts about Ebola Hemorrhagic Fever. (EHF)

Ebola (EHF) is a highly infectious disease caused by an infinitely small virus, which can only be observed under an electron microscope. The wriggling thread looks like a child's scribble or a miniscule snake, convoluted and in places twisted round on itself. Being so tiny the virus can easily penetrate cells of body fluids so the disease is transmitted by contact with infected liquids – (sneezes, coughs, blood, breast milk, spittle, semen) – or by eating infected food. Once inside a victim the virus makes blood cells expand till they burst, thus causing bleeding both internally and through external orifices. That's why Ebola is called a hemorrhagic fever.

EHF affects man, duikers, monkeys, porcupines, apes (e.g. chimpanzees, bonobos, gorillas) and other animals. Possibly over 5,000 gorillas had died of EHF by early 2015. Usually death in humans occurs soon after the appearance of headaches, body pains, diarrhoea and vomiting. These symptoms are followed by liver and kidney malfunction. Death is often due to low blood pressure caused by losses of body fluids.

The natural reservoir for the illness is not yet established but bats are the chief suspects. They – as well as pigs, dogs, and some rodents – show no symptoms but carry antibodies. Other possible carriers are plants, arthropods and birds. **(An arthropod** is an invertebrate animal having an external skeleton, a segmented body, and jointed appendages.) Bats in Asia have been found to carry Ebola antibodies but so far there have been no (recorded) appearances of EHF there.

There are four known types of Ebola. Of these three affect humans.

Outbreaks occur intermittently in tropical sub-Sahara regions, and EHF must have been endemic to Africa, and probably to Asia, long before it was first investigated in 1976 when the antibodies were recognised in bats living in a Congolese cotton factory. Since then outbreaks have erupted in the Democratic Republic of Congo, Gabon, Ivory Coast, The Republic of Congo, Sudan, and Uganda. During 2014 there were vast epidemics in Sierra Leone, Liberia and Guinea. In early 2015 the disease was still killing people in Sierra Leon, but the outbreak is now being brought under control.

EHF was first studied in 1976 near Station d'Epulu – where in 1971 we almost camped. No researcher was keen to have the frightful illness called after him/her so it was given the name of the local river.

W.H.O. reported:

During 2013:	24 outbreaks produced 1716 cases.
By 15 October 2014:	17 cases *outside Africa* caused 4 deaths.
By 18 December 2014:	19,078 cases had caused 7,413 deaths.

In 2014 four health workers who caught Ebola in Africa were repatriated to the USA, Britain and to Spain where they received the best possible intensive care with oral and intravenous rehydration techniques supplemented with specific treatment against the various symptoms. One of those sufferers died. The other three pulled through but in Africa itself the 2014-15 outbreak has killed 11,000 people so far (May 2015). People who have recovered are immune to further attacks but still carry the virus for up to several weeks or even months.

Currently there is no known cure for the illness, and no particular treatment or vaccine against EHF is commercially available; but studies are being undertaken of a number of potential methods for fighting the disease.

The Euro Weekly News of 11-17 Dec 2014 – an English periodical sold in Spain, carried the story that is summarised below. It illustrates the terror induced by Ebola.

A Nigerian traveller arriving at a Spanish airport fell to the floor, obviously unwell. People were so afraid that he might have Ebola that no one attempted to succour him and after fifty minutes he died. He was not suffering from Ebola but collapsed when packets of illegal drugs, which he was carrying, broke inside his intestines. He had arrived from Turkey – not from Africa.

Luckily it would be difficult to use EHF as a weapon of mass destruction because the virus rapidly becomes ineffective when exposed to air, though it can survive in a dried state on surfaces for a few hours and in body fluids for a few days. It can be killed with chlorine and boiling.

****

These facts have been collected from various sources: documentaries on several English, French and Spanish TV channels, newspaper articles, the Internet and talks.

51. Guenon monkeys.

The following ABC poem may amuse you.

<u>The Missed Meal</u>

In the jungle, branch to bough
jumping monkeys – scared – avoid
killing claws of climbing cat.
Lighter, they can scamper higher...
mocking downwards as they scat.

In the canopies of Congo
jitt'ring Guenons – proud – escape.
Kindling spits, and vengeance bent,
leopard, hungry, cross, frustrated,
makes a swishing-tail descent.

An ABC Poem has verses with 5 lines. The first four lines of each stanza start with sequential letters of the alphabet. (In this case with I, J, K, L) The fifth line can begin with any letter. Rhymes may, but need not, be included.

In colloquial language to 'scat' means to 'b----r off'.
An animal dropping is also technically called a 'scat', so in the poem the word has an allusion to the diarrhoea that the monkeys suffer in their panic as they b----r off.

Jitt'ring means jittering about in fear from branch to branch, and also jittery – i.e. frightened.

<u>A **B**ounty of **B**'s</u>

It is astonishing how many settlements, villages and towns that we went through had names starting with **B**.

Bouar

Bombasele 1 and **B**ombasele 2

Boali

Bambari

Bangui

Bangassou

Those top 7 are in Central African Republic.

Now we are in Zaire:

Bondo

Buta

Bobenge

Banali

Then there's region simply jam packed full of **B**'s.
Here are just *a few* of them:
Bengamisa **B**afwapuda **B**afwabali **B**atama **B**afwakwandji **B**angum **B**utembo

Buna

Beni

Bukavu

Bujumbura in **B**urundi

Also, of course, we started from **B**lantyre! (Malawi) – and now we've reached the end of this book.

****

45355450R00117

Made in the USA
Charleston, SC
18 August 2015